MznLnx

Missing Links Exam Preps

Exam Prep for

Advanced Accounting

Jeter & Chaney, 2nd Edition

The MznLnx Exam Prep is your link from the texbook and lecture to your exams.
The MznLnx Exam Preps are unauthorized and comprehensive reviews of your textbooks.

All material provided by MznLnx and Rico Publications (c) 2010
Textbook publishers and textbook authors do not particpate in or contribute to these reviews.

MznLnx

Rico Publications

Exam Prep for Advanced Accounting
2nd Edition
Jeter & Chaney

Publisher: Raymond Houge
Assistant Editor: Michael Rouger
Text and Cover Designer: Lisa Buckner
Marketing Manager: Sara Swagger
Project Manager, Editorial Production: Jerry Emerson
Art Director: Vernon Lowerui

Product Manager: Dave Mason
Editorial Assitant: Rachel Guzmanji
Pedagogy: Debra Long
Cover Image: Jim Reed/Getty Images
Text and Cover Printer: City Printing, Inc.
Compositor: Media Mix, Inc.

(c) 2010 Rico Publications
ALL RIGHTS RESERVED. No part of this work covered by the copyright may be reproduced or used in any form or by an means--graphic, electronic, or mechanical, including photocopying, recording, taping, Web distribution, information storage, and retrieval systems, or in any other manner--without the written permission of the publisher.

Printed in the United States
ISBN:

For more information about our products, contact us at:
Dave.Mason@RicoPublications.com

For permission to use material from this text or product, submit a request online to:
Dave.Mason@RicoPublications.com

Contents

CHAPTER 1
Introduction to Business Combinations — 1

CHAPTER 2
Accounting for Business Combinations — 8

CHAPTER 3
Consolidated Financial Statements-Date of Acquisition, — 14

CHAPTER 4
Consolidated Financial Statements After Acquisition — 20

CHAPTER 5
Allocation and Depreciation of Differences Between Cost and Book Values — 24

CHAPTER 6
Elimination of Unrealized Profit on Intercompany Sales of Inventory — 30

CHAPTER 7
Elimination of Unrealized Gains or Losses on Intercompany Sales — 33

CHAPTER 8
Changes in Ownership Interest — 36

CHAPTER 9
Intercompany Bond Holdings and Miscellaneous Topics — 38

CHAPTER 10
Insolvency—Liquidation and Reorganization — 41

CHAPTER 11
International Accounting and the Global Economy — 46

CHAPTER 12
Accounting for Foreign Currency Transactions and Hedging Foreign Exchange Risk — 54

CHAPTER 13
Translation of Financial Statements of Foreign Affiliates — 61

CHAPTER 14
Reporting for Segments and for Interim Financial Periods — 65

CHAPTER 15
Partnerships: Formation, Operation, and Ownership Changes — 71

CHAPTER 16
Partnership Liquidation — 75

CHAPTER 17
Introduction to Fund Accounting — 76

CHAPTER 18
Introduction to Accounting for State and Local Governmental Units — 81

CHAPTER 19
Accounting for Nongovernment Nonbusiness Organizations — 86

ANSWER KEY — 104

TO THE STUDENT

COMPREHENSIVE

The *MznLnx* Exam Prep series is designed to help you pass your exams. Editors at MznLnx review your textbooks and then prepare these practice exams to help you master the textbook material. Unlike study guides, workbooks, and practice tests provided by the texbook publisher and textbook authors, *MznLnx* gives you **all** of the material in each chapter in exam form, not just samples, so you can be sure to nail your exam.

MECHANICAL

The MznLnx Exam Prep series creates exams that will help you learn the subject matter as well as test you on your understanding. Each question is designed to help you master the concept. Just working through the exams, you gain an understanding of the subject--its a simple mechanical process that produces success.

INTEGRATED STUDY GUIDE AND REVIEW

MznLnx is not just a set of exams designed to test you, its also a comprehensive review of the subject content. Each exam question is also a review of the concept, making sure that you will get the answer correct without having to go to other sources of material. You learn as you go! Its the easiest way to pass an exam.

HUMOR

Studying can be tedious and dry. MznLnx's instructional design includes moderate humor within the exam questions on occassion, to break the tedium and revitalize the brain

Chapter 1. Introduction to Business Combinations 1

1. The _____ is a private, not-for-profit organization whose primary purpose is to develop generally accepted accounting principles (GAAP) within the United States in the public's interest. The Securities and Exchange Commission (SEC) designated the _____ as the organization responsible for setting accounting standards for public companies in the U.S. It was created in 1973, replacing the Accounting Principles Board and the Committee on Accounting Procedure of the American Institute of Certified Public Accountants. The _____'s mission is 'to establish and improve standards of financial accounting and reporting for the guidance and education of the public, including issuers, auditors, and users of financial information.'

The _____ is not a governmental body.

   a. Fannie Mae
   c. Public company
   b. Governmental Accounting Standards Board
   d. Financial Accounting Standards Board

2. The _____ is an independent agency of the United States government, established in 1914 by the _____ Act. Its principal mission is the promotion of 'consumer protection' and the elimination and prevention of what regulators perceive to be harmfully 'anti-competitive' business practices, such as coercive monopoly.

The _____ Act was one of President Wilson's major acts against trusts.

   a. BMC Software, Inc.
   c. Federal Trade Commission
   b. BNSF Railway
   d. 3M Company

3. In economics and finance, _____ is the change in total cost that arises when the quantity produced changes by one unit. It is the cost of producing one more unit of a good. Mathematically, the _____ function is expressed as the first derivative of the total cost (TC) function with respect to quantity (Q.)

   a. Variable cost
   c. Cost accounting
   b. Cost of quality
   d. Marginal cost

4. In economics, business, retail, and accounting, a _____ is the value of money that has been used up to produce something, and hence is not available for use anymore. In economics, a _____ is an alternative that is given up as a result of a decision. In business, the _____ may be one of acquisition, in which case the amount of money expended to acquire it is counted as _____.

   a. Prime cost
   c. Cost allocation
   b. Cost of quality
   d. Cost

5. A _____ occurs when a financial sponsor acquires a controlling interest in a company's equity and where a significant percentage of the purchase price is financed through leverage (borrowing.) The assets of the acquired company are used as collateral for the borrowed capital, sometimes with assets of the acquiring company. The bonds or other paper issued for a _____ is commonly considered not to be investment grade because of the significant risks involved.

   a. 3M Company
   c. Leveraged buyout
   b. BMC Software, Inc.
   d. BNSF Railway

Chapter 1. Introduction to Business Combinations

6. An _____ is a term used in behavioral economics to describe those types of behaviors that impose costs on a person in the long-run that are not taken into account when making decisions in the present. Classical Economics discourages government from creating legislation that targets internalities, because it is assumed that the consumer takes these personal costs into account when paying for the good that causes the _____. For example, cigarettes should be taxed because of the negative consumption externalities that they impose, such as second-hand smoke, not because the smoker harms him or herself by smoking.

   a. Operating budget
   b. Inventory turnover ratio
   c. Authorised capital
   d. Internality

7. In economics, a _____ is a lower rated, potentially higher paying bond.

   - High-yield debt

   A high-risk, non-investment-grade bond with a low credit rating, usually BB or lower; as a consequence, it usually has a high yield. opposite of investment-grade bond. This content can be found on the following page:

   a. BNSF Railway
   b. 3M Company
   c. BMC Software, Inc.
   d. Junk bond

8. In business or economics a _____ is a combination of two companies into one larger company. Such actions are commonly voluntary and involve stock swap or cash payment to the target. Stock swap is often used as it allows the shareholders of the two companies to share the risk involved in the deal. A _____ can resemble a takeover but result in a new company name (often combining the names of the original companies) and in new branding; in some cases, terming the combination a '_____' rather than an acquisition is done purely for political or marketing reasons.

   a. BMC Software, Inc.
   b. BNSF Railway
   c. 3M Company
   d. Merger

9. In finance, a _____ is a debt security, in which the authorized issuer owes the holders a debt and, depending on the terms of the _____, is obliged to pay interest (the coupon) and/or to repay the principal at a later date, termed maturity. It is a formal contract to repay borrowed money with interest at fixed intervals.

   Thus a _____ is like a loan: the issuer is the borrower, the _____ holder is the lender, and the coupon is the interest.

   a. Bond
   b. Zero-coupon bond
   c. Coupon rate
   d. Revenue bonds

10. In law, _____ refers to the process by which a company (or part of a company) is brought to an end, and the assets and property of the company redistributed. _____ can also be referred to as winding-up or dissolution, although dissolution technically refers to the last stage of _____. The process of _____ also arises when customs, an authority or agency in a country responsible for collecting and safeguarding customs duties, determines the final computation or ascertainment of the duties or drawback accruing on an entry.

    a. 3M Company
    b. BMC Software, Inc.
    c. Bankruptcy protection
    d. Liquidation

Chapter 1. Introduction to Business Combinations

11. In microeconomics and management, the term _____ describes a style of management control. Vertically integrated companies are united through a hierarchy with a common owner. Usually each member of the hierarchy produces a different product or (market-specific) service, and the products combine to satisfy a common need.
    a. Vertical integration
    b. BMC Software, Inc.
    c. 3M Company
    d. BNSF Railway

12. An _____ is the buying of one company by another. An _____ may be friendly or hostile. In the former case, the companies cooperate in negotiations; in the latter case, the takeover target is unwilling to be bought or the target's board has no prior knowledge of the offer. _____ usually refers to a purchase of a smaller firm by a larger one. Sometimes, however, a smaller firm will acquire management control of a larger or longer established company and keep its name for the combined entity. This is known as a reverse takeover.
    a. AMEX
    b. ABC Television Network
    c. AIG
    d. Acquisition

13. In business and accounting, _____ are everything of value that is owned by a person or company. It is a claim on the property your income of a borrower. The balance sheet of a firm records the monetary value of the _____ owned by the firm.
    a. Accrual basis accounting
    b. Earnings before interest, taxes, depreciation and amortization
    c. Accounts receivable
    d. Assets

14. There are many _____ entity defined in the legal systems of various countries. These include corporations, partnerships, sole traders and other specialized types of organization. Some of these types are listed below, by country.
    a. Staple right
    b. Bond indenture
    c. Hospital Survey and Construction Act
    d. Types of Business

15. The _____ is the former authoritative body of the American Institute of Certified Public Accountants (AICPA.) It was created by the American Institute of Certified Public Accountants in 1959 and issued pronouncements on accounting principles until 1973, when it was replaced by the Financial Accounting Standards Board (FASB.)

    The _____ was disbanded in the hopes that the smaller, fully-independent FASB could more effectively create accounting standards.

    a. Institute of Management Accountants
    b. International Federation of Accountants
    c. American Payroll Association
    d. Accounting Principles Board

16. _____ were published by Accounting Principles Board (APB.) The board was created by American Institute of Certified Public Accountants (AICPA) in 1959 and was replaced by Financial Accounting Standards Board (FASB) in 1973. Its mission was to develop an overall conceptual framework of US generally accepted accounting principles (US GAAP.)
    a. AMEX
    b. AIG
    c. ABC Television Network
    d. Accounting Principles Board Opinions

17. _____ is a term used for a number of concepts involving either the performance of an investigation of a business or person, or the performance of an act with a certain standard of care. It can be a legal obligation, but the term will more commonly apply to voluntary investigations. A common example of _____ in various industries is the process through which a potential acquirer evaluates a target company or its assets for acquisition.

a. Due diligence
b. Tax patent
c. Burden of proof
d. Negligence

18. In financial accounting, a _____ is defined as an obligation of an entity arising from past transactions or events, the settlement of which may result in the transfer or use of assets, provision of services or other yielding of economic benefits in the future.
    a. Liability
    b. False Claims Act
    c. Corporate governance
    d. Vested

19. _____ are sometimes the same as net worth, or shareholders' equity - assets minus liabilities. The term _____ is commonly used with charities or not for profit entities. Although these entities don't make money, it is important to maintain reasonable reserves to help future growth.
    a. Net interest spread
    b. Sortino ratio
    c. Net assets
    d. Debtor days

20. A _____ or chief executive is one of the highest-ranking corporate officer (executive) or administrator in charge of total management. An individual selected as President and _____ of a corporation, company, organization, or agency, reports to the board of directors. In internal communication and press releases, many companies capitalize the term and those of other high positions, even when they are not proper nouns.
    a. Kohlberg Kravis Roberts ' Co
    b. Return on equity
    c. Chief executive officer
    d. Return on assets

21. In accounting, _____ has a very specific meaning. It is an outflow of cash or other valuable assets from a person or company to another person or company. This outflow of cash is generally one side of a trade for products or services that have equal or better current or future value to the buyer than to the seller.
    a. Expense
    b. AIG
    c. AMEX
    d. ABC Television Network

22. _____ in economics and business is the result of an exchange and from that trade we assign a numerical monetary value to a good, service or asset. If Alice trades Bob 4 apples for an orange, the _____ of an orange is 4 apples. Inversely, the _____ of an apple is 1/4 oranges.
    a. Price discrimination
    b. Transactional Net Margin Method
    c. Discounts and allowances
    d. Price

23. A _____ is a fungible, negotiable instrument representing financial value. they are broadly categorized into debt securities (such as banknotes, bonds and debentures), and equity securities; e.g., common stocks. The company or other entity issuing the _____ is called the issuer.
    a. Tracking stock
    b. BMC Software, Inc.
    c. Security
    d. 3M Company

24. A _____, (formerly a securities exchange) is a corporation or mutual organization which provides 'trading' facilities for stock brokers and traders, to trade stocks and other securities. _____s also provide facilities for the issue and redemption of securities as well as other financial instruments and capital events including the payment of income and dividends. The securities traded on a _____ include: shares issued by companies, unit trusts, derivatives, pooled investment products and bonds.

Chapter 1. Introduction to Business Combinations

a. BNSF Railway
b. 3M Company
c. Stock exchange
d. BMC Software, Inc.

25. The term _____ or replacement value refers to the amount that an entity would have to pay, at the present time, to replace any one of its assets.

In the insurance industry, '_____' is a method of computing the value of an item insured. _____ is not market value, but is instead the cost to replace an item or structure at its pre-loss condition.

a. Channel stuffing
b. Consolidated financial statements
c. Time and motion study
d. Replacement cost

26. _____ is the calculated approximation of a result which is usable even if input data may be incomplete or uncertain.

In statistics, see _____ theory, estimator.

In mathematics, approximation or _____ typically means finding upper or lower bounds of a quantity that cannot readily be computed precisely and is also an educated guess.

a. AMEX
b. AIG
c. Estimation
d. ABC Television Network

27. In finance, _____ is the process of estimating the potential market value of a financial asset or liability. They can be done on assets (for example, investments in marketable securities such as stocks, options, business enterprises, or intangible assets such as patents and trademarks) or on liabilities (e.g., Bonds issued by a company.) A _____ is required in many contexts including investment analysis, capital budgeting, merger and acquisition transactions, financial reporting, taxable events to determine the proper tax liability, and in litigation.

a. Vyborg Appeal
b. Disclosure
c. Valuation
d. Daybook

28. _____ is a specific term used in companies' financial reporting from the company-whole point of view. Because that use excludes the effects of changing ownership interest, an economic measure of _____ is necessary for financial analysis from the shareholders' point of view

_____ is defined by the Financial Accounting Standards Board, or FASB, as 'the change in equity [net assets] of a business enterprise during a period from transactions and other events and circumstances from nonowner sources. It includes all changes in equity during a period except those resulting from investments by owners and distributions to owners.'

_____ is the sum of net income and other items that must bypass the income statement because they have not been realized, including items like an unrealized holding gain or loss from available for sale securities and foreign currency translation gains or losses.

Chapter 1. Introduction to Business Combinations

    a. BNSF Railway   b. 3M Company
    c. BMC Software, Inc.   d. Comprehensive income

29. _____ are financial statements that factor the holding company's subsidiaries into its aggregated accounting figure. It is a representation of how the holding company is doing as a group. The consolidated accounts should provide a true and fair view of the financial and operating conditions of the group.

    a. Replacement cost   b. Consolidated financial statements
    c. Redemption value   d. Committee on Accounting Procedure

30. In an economy, production, consumption and exchange are carried out by two basic _____: the firm and the household.

    a. ABC Television Network   b. Economic units
    c. AMEX   d. AIG

31. A _____ is a company that owns enough voting stock in another firm to control management and operations by influencing or electing its board of directors; the second company being deemed as a subsidiary of the _____. The definition of a _____ differs from jurisdiction to jurisdiction, with the definition normally being defined by way of laws dealing with companies in that jurisdiction.

The _____-subsidiary company relationship is defined by Part 1.2, Division 6, Section 46 of the Corporations Act 2001 (Cth), which states:

A body corporate (in this section called the first body) is a subsidiary of another body corporate if, and only if:

    (a) the other body:

        (i) controls the composition of the first body's board; or

        (ii) is in a position to cast, or control the casting of, more than one-half of the maximum number of votes that might be cast at a general meeting of the first body; or

        (iii) holds more than one-half of the issued share capital of the first body (excluding any part of that issued share capital that carries no right to participate beyond a specified amount in a distribution of either profits or capital); or

    (b) the first body is a subsidiary of a subsidiary of the other body.

    a. Subsidiary   b. 3M Company
    c. BMC Software, Inc.   d. Parent company

32. In financial accounting, a _____ or statement of financial position is a summary of a person's or organization's balances. Assets, liabilities and ownership equity are listed as of a specific date, such as the end of its financial year. A _____ is often described as a snapshot of a company's financial condition.

Chapter 1. Introduction to Business Combinations 7

   a. Balance sheet
   c. Financial statements
   b. 3M Company
   d. Statement of retained earnings

33. _____ are formal records of a business' financial activities.

In British English, including United Kingdom company law, _____ are often referred to as accounts, although the term _____ is also used, particularly by accountants.

_____ provide an overview of a business' financial condition in both short and long term.

   a. Financial statements
   c. 3M Company
   b. Notes to the financial statements
   d. Statement of retained earnings

34. _____ is a fee paid on borrowed assets. It is the price paid for the use of borrowed money, or, money earned by deposited funds. Assets that are sometimes lent with _____ include money, shares, consumer goods through hire purchase, major assets such as aircraft, and even entire factories in finance lease arrangements. The _____ is calculated upon the value of the assets in the same manner as upon money.
   a. ABC Television Network
   c. Insolvency
   b. AIG
   d. Interest

35. _____ is equal to the income that a firm has after subtracting costs and expenses from the total revenue. _____ can be distributed among holders of common stock as a dividend or held by the firm as retained earnings.

The items deducted will typically include tax expense, financing expense (interest expense), and minority interest. Likewise, preferred stock dividends will be subtracted too, though they are not an expense.

   a. Matching principle
   c. Long-term liabilities
   b. Net income
   d. Generally accepted accounting principles

Chapter 2. Accounting for Business Combinations

1. The _____ is the former authoritative body of the American Institute of Certified Public Accountants (AICPA.) It was created by the American Institute of Certified Public Accountants in 1959 and issued pronouncements on accounting principles until 1973, when it was replaced by the Financial Accounting Standards Board (FASB.)

   The _____ was disbanded in the hopes that the smaller, fully-independent FASB could more effectively create accounting standards.

   a. Institute of Management Accountants
   b. American Payroll Association
   c. International Federation of Accountants
   d. Accounting Principles Board

2. _____ were published by Accounting Principles Board (APB.) The board was created by American Institute of Certified Public Accountants (AICPA) in 1959 and was replaced by Financial Accounting Standards Board (FASB) in 1973. Its mission was to develop an overall conceptual framework of US generally accepted accounting principles (US GAAP.)

   a. Accounting Principles Board Opinions
   b. ABC Television Network
   c. AMEX
   d. AIG

3. _____ is the process of increasing, or accounting for, an amount over a period of time. Particular instances of the term include:

   - _____, the allocation of a lump sum amount to different time periods, particularly for loans and other forms of finance, including related interest or other finance charges.
     - _____ schedule, a table detailing each periodic payment on a loan (typically a mortgage), as generated by an _____ calculator.
     - Negative _____, an _____ schedule where the loan amount actually increases through not paying the full interest
   - Amortized analysis, analyzing the execution cost of algorithms over a sequence of operations.
   - _____ of capital expenditures of certain assets under accounting rules, particularly intangible assets, in a manner analogous to depreciation.
   - _____

   a. EBIT
   b. Annuity
   c. Amortization
   d. Intangible

4. _____ is a fee paid on borrowed assets. It is the price paid for the use of borrowed money, or, money earned by deposited funds. Assets that are sometimes lent with _____ include money, shares, consumer goods through hire purchase, major assets such as aircraft, and even entire factories in finance lease arrangements. The _____ is calculated upon the value of the assets in the same manner as upon money.

   a. AIG
   b. Insolvency
   c. Interest
   d. ABC Television Network

5. The _____ is currently the source of generally accepted accounting principles (GAAP) used by State and Local governments in the [[United States of America]]. As with most of the entities involved in creating GAAP in the United States, it is a private, non-governmental organization.

   The _____ is subject to oversight by the Financial Accounting Foundation (FAF), which selects the members of the _____ and the Financial Accounting Standards Board, and funds both organizations.

Chapter 2. Accounting for Business Combinations

a. Fannie Mae

c. Governmental Accounting Standards Board

b. Multinational corporation

d. National Conference of Commissioners on Uniform State Laws

6. _____ means the giving out of information, either voluntarily or to be in compliance with legal regulations or workplace rules.

- In Computer security, full _____ means disclosing full information about vulnerabilities.
- In computing, _____ widget
- Journalism, full _____ refers to disclosing the interests of the writer which may bear on the subject being written about, for example, if the writer has worked with an interview subject in the past.

- In law:
    - The law of England and Wales, _____ refers to a process that may form part of legal proceedings, whereby parties inform to other parties the existence of any relevant documents that are, or have been, in their control. This compares with the process known as discovery in the course of legal proceedings in the United States.
    - In U.S. civil procedure (litigation rules for civil cases), _____ is a stage prior to trial. In civil cases, each party must disclose to the opposing party the following: names of witnesses which it may use to support its side, copies of documents (or mere description of these documents) in its control which it may use to support its side, computation of damages claimed, and certain insurance information. _____ is related to, but technically prior to, the discovery stage.
    - In Company law (known as 'corporate law' in the United States), _____ refers to giving out information about public or limited companies or their officers, which might be kept secret if the company was a private company or a partnership.

- In real property transactions, _____ refers to providing to a buyer information known to the seller or broker/agent concerning the condition or other aspects of real property that would affect the property's value or desirability. These rules regarding what information must be disclosed, and whether the information must be disclosed even if a buyer does not ask, vary from one jurisdiction to the next.

a. Controlled Foreign Corporations

c. Trailing

b. Tax harmonisation

d. Disclosure

7. _____ are sometimes the same as net worth, or shareholders' equity - assets minus liabilities. The term _____ is commonly used with charities or not for profit entities. Although these entities don't make money, it is important to maintain reasonable reserves to help future growth.

a. Net assets

c. Net interest spread

b. Sortino ratio

d. Debtor days

8. In business and accounting, _____ are everything of value that is owned by a person or company. It is a claim on the property your income of a borrower. The balance sheet of a firm records the monetary value of the _____ owned by the firm.

Chapter 2. Accounting for Business Combinations

a. Earnings before interest, taxes, depreciation and amortization
b. Assets
c. Accounts receivable
d. Accrual basis accounting

9. An _____ is the buying of one company by another. An _____ may be friendly or hostile. In the former case, the companies cooperate in negotiations; in the latter case, the takeover target is unwilling to be bought or the target's board has no prior knowledge of the offer. _____ usually refers to a purchase of a smaller firm by a larger one. Sometimes, however, a smaller firm will acquire management control of a larger or longer established company and keep its name for the combined entity. This is known as a reverse takeover.

a. AIG
b. ABC Television Network
c. Acquisition
d. AMEX

10. In accounting, _____ has a very specific meaning. It is an outflow of cash or other valuable assets from a person or company to another person or company. This outflow of cash is generally one side of a trade for products or services that have equal or better current or future value to the buyer than to the seller.

a. ABC Television Network
b. AIG
c. Expense
d. AMEX

11. A _____ is a fungible, negotiable instrument representing financial value. they are broadly categorized into debt securities (such as banknotes, bonds and debentures), and equity securities; e.g., common stocks. The company or other entity issuing the _____ is called the issuer.

a. Tracking stock
b. Security
c. 3M Company
d. BMC Software, Inc.

12. In economics, business, retail, and accounting, a _____ is the value of money that has been used up to produce something, and hence is not available for use anymore. In economics, a _____ is an alternative that is given up as a result of a decision. In business, the _____ may be one of acquisition, in which case the amount of money expended to acquire it is counted as _____.

a. Prime cost
b. Cost allocation
c. Cost of quality
d. Cost

13. _____, in law and economics, is a form of risk management primarily used to hedge against the risk of a contingent loss. _____ is defined as the equitable transfer of the risk of a loss, from one entity to another, in exchange for a premium, and can be thought of as a guaranteed small loss to prevent a large, possibly devastating loss. An insurer is a company selling the _____; an insured is the person or entity buying the _____.

a. Insurance
b. ABC Television Network
c. AMEX
d. AIG

14. The term _____ is a term applied to practices that are perfunctory, or seek to satisfy the minimum requirements or to conform to a convention or doctrine. It has different meanings in different fields.

In accounting, _____ earnings are those earnings of companies in addition to actual earnings calculated under the Generally Accepted Accounting Principles (GAAP) in their quarterly and yearly financial reports.

Chapter 2. Accounting for Business Combinations

a. Bottom line
b. Treasury stock
c. Payroll
d. Pro forma

15. _____ are formal records of a business' financial activities.

In British English, including United Kingdom company law, _____ are often referred to as accounts, although the term _____ is also used, particularly by accountants.

_____ provide an overview of a business' financial condition in both short and long term.

a. Financial statements
b. Notes to the financial statements
c. 3M Company
d. Statement of retained earnings

16. _____ were documents issued by the Committee on Accounting Procedure between 1938 and 1959 on various accounting problems. They were discontinued with the dissolution of the Committee in 1959 under a recommendation from the Special Committee on Research Program. In all, 51 bulletins were issued, however, the lack of binding authority over AICPA's membership reduced the influence of, and compliance with the content of the bulletins.

a. AIG
b. ABC Television Network
c. Other postemployment benefits
d. Accounting Research Bulletins

17. The _____ founded on April 1, 2001 is the successor of the International Accounting Standards Committee (IASC) founded in June 1973 in London. It is responsible for developing the International Financial Reporting Standards (new name for the International Accounting Standards issued after 2001), and promoting the use and application of these standards.

The _____ is an independent, privately-funded accounting standard-setter based in London, UK.

a. Information Systems Audit and Control Association
b. Emerging technologies
c. Institute of Management Accountants
d. International Accounting Standards Board

18. The phrase _____, according to the Organization for Economic Co-operation and Development, refers to 'creative work undertaken on a systematic basis in order to increase the stock of knowledge, including knowledge of man, culture and society, and the use of this stock of knowledge to devise new applications [sic]'

New product design and development is more than often a crucial factor in the survival of a company. In an industry that is fast changing, firms must continually revise their design and range of products. This is necessary due to continuous technology change and development as well as other competitors and the changing preference of customers.

a. BMC Software, Inc.
b. BNSF Railway
c. 3M Company
d. Research and development

19. _____, in accrual accounting, is any account where the asset or liability is not realized until a future date (accounting period), e.g. annuities, charges, taxes, income, etc. The _____ item may be carried, dependent on type of deferral, as either an asset or liability.

a. Deferred
b. Cash basis accounting
c. Payroll
d. Pro forma

20. _____ is an accounting concept, meaning a future tax liability or asset, resulting from temporary differences between book (accounting) value of assets and liabilities and their tax value, or timing differences between the recognition of gains and losses in financial statements and their recognition in a tax computation.

Temporary differences are differences between the carrying amount of an asset or liability recognised in the balance sheet and the amount attributed to that asset or liability for tax purposes (the tax base.)

a. Tax refund
b. Federal tax revenue by state
c. Deficit
d. Deferred tax

21. The _____ is a private, not-for-profit organization whose primary purpose is to develop generally accepted accounting principles (GAAP) within the United States in the public's interest. The Securities and Exchange Commission (SEC) designated the _____ as the organization responsible for setting accounting standards for public companies in the U.S. It was created in 1973, replacing the Accounting Principles Board and the Committee on Accounting Procedure of the American Institute of Certified Public Accountants. The _____'s mission is 'to establish and improve standards of financial accounting and reporting for the guidance and education of the public, including issuers, auditors, and users of financial information.'

The _____ is not a governmental body.

a. Public company
b. Governmental Accounting Standards Board
c. Fannie Mae
d. Financial Accounting Standards Board

22. An _____ is a tax levied on the financial income of people, corporations, or other legal entities. Various _____ systems exist, with varying degrees of tax incidence. Income taxation can be progressive, proportional, or regressive.

a. Income tax
b. Implied level of government service
c. Individual Retirement Arrangement
d. Ordinary income

23. _____ is a specific term used in companies' financial reporting from the company-whole point of view. Because that use excludes the effects of changing ownership interest, an economic measure of _____ is necessary for financial analysis from the shareholders' point of view

_____ is defined by the Financial Accounting Standards Board, or FASB, as 'the change in equity [net assets] of a business enterprise during a period from transactions and other events and circumstances from nonowner sources. It includes all changes in equity during a period except those resulting from investments by owners and distributions to owners.'

_____ is the sum of net income and other items that must bypass the income statement because they have not been realized, including items like an unrealized holding gain or loss from available for sale securities and foreign currency translation gains or losses.

Chapter 2. Accounting for Business Combinations

a. BNSF Railway
c. Comprehensive income
b. 3M Company
d. BMC Software, Inc.

24. _____ in economics and business is the result of an exchange and from that trade we assign a numerical monetary value to a good, service or asset. If Alice trades Bob 4 apples for an orange, the _____ of an orange is 4 apples. Inversely, the _____ of an apple is 1/4 oranges.
   a. Price
   c. Transactional Net Margin Method
   b. Price discrimination
   d. Discounts and allowances

25. A _____ occurs when a financial sponsor acquires a controlling interest in a company's equity and where a significant percentage of the purchase price is financed through leverage (borrowing.) The assets of the acquired company are used as collateral for the borrowed capital, sometimes with assets of the acquiring company. The bonds or other paper issued for a _____ is commonly considered not to be investment grade because of the significant risks involved.
   a. BNSF Railway
   c. Leveraged buyout
   b. 3M Company
   d. BMC Software, Inc.

Chapter 3. Consolidated Financial Statements-Date of Acquisition,

1. In business and accounting, _____ are everything of value that is owned by a person or company. It is a claim on the property your income of a borrower. The balance sheet of a firm records the monetary value of the _____ owned by the firm.

   a. Accrual basis accounting
   b. Earnings before interest, taxes, depreciation and amortization
   c. Accounts receivable
   d. Assets

2. The _____ is a private, not-for-profit organization whose primary purpose is to develop generally accepted accounting principles (GAAP) within the United States in the public's interest. The Securities and Exchange Commission (SEC) designated the _____ as the organization responsible for setting accounting standards for public companies in the U.S. It was created in 1973, replacing the Accounting Principles Board and the Committee on Accounting Procedure of the American Institute of Certified Public Accountants. The _____'s mission is 'to establish and improve standards of financial accounting and reporting for the guidance and education of the public, including issuers, auditors, and users of financial information.'

   The _____ is not a governmental body.

   a. Financial Accounting Standards Board
   b. Governmental Accounting Standards Board
   c. Fannie Mae
   d. Public company

3. A _____ is a company that owns enough voting stock in another firm to control management and operations by influencing or electing its board of directors; the second company being deemed as a subsidiary of the _____. The definition of a _____ differs from jurisdiction to jurisdiction, with the definition normally being defined by way of laws dealing with companies in that jurisdiction.

   The _____-subsidiary company relationship is defined by Part 1.2, Division 6, Section 46 of the Corporations Act 2001 (Cth), which states:

   A body corporate (in this section called the first body) is a subsidiary of another body corporate if, and only if:

   (a) the other body:

   (i) controls the composition of the first body's board; or

   (ii) is in a position to cast, or control the casting of, more than one-half of the maximum number of votes that might be cast at a general meeting of the first body; or

   (iii) holds more than one-half of the issued share capital of the first body (excluding any part of that issued share capital that carries no right to participate beyond a specified amount in a distribution of either profits or capital); or

   (b) the first body is a subsidiary of a subsidiary of the other body.

   a. Subsidiary
   b. 3M Company
   c. BMC Software, Inc.
   d. Parent company

Chapter 3. Consolidated Financial Statements-Date of Acquisition,

4. A _____, in business matters, is an entity that is controlled by a bigger and more powerful entity. The controlled entity is called a company, corporation, or limited liability company, and the controlling entity is called its parent (or the parent company.) The reason for this distinction is that a lone company cannot be a _____ of any organization; only an entity representing a legal fiction as a separate entity can be a _____.
   a. BMC Software, Inc.
   b. 3M Company
   c. Parent company
   d. Subsidiary

5. An _____ is the buying of one company by another. An _____ may be friendly or hostile. In the former case, the companies cooperate in negotiations; in the latter case, the takeover target is unwilling to be bought or the target's board has no prior knowledge of the offer. _____ usually refers to a purchase of a smaller firm by a larger one. Sometimes, however, a smaller firm will acquire management control of a larger or longer established company and keep its name for the combined entity. This is known as a reverse takeover.
   a. AIG
   b. ABC Television Network
   c. AMEX
   d. Acquisition

6. _____ is a fee paid on borrowed assets. It is the price paid for the use of borrowed money , or, money earned by deposited funds .Assets that are sometimes lent with _____ include money, shares, consumer goods through hire purchase, major assets such as aircraft, and even entire factories in finance lease arrangements. The _____ is calculated upon the value of the assets in the same manner as upon money.
   a. AIG
   b. ABC Television Network
   c. Insolvency
   d. Interest

7. _____ is the process of increasing, or accounting for, an amount over a period of time. Particular instances of the term include:

   - _____, the allocation of a lump sum amount to different time periods, particularly for loans and other forms of finance, including related interest or other finance charges.
     - _____ schedule, a table detailing each periodic payment on a loan (typically a mortgage), as generated by an _____ calculator.
     - Negative _____, an _____ schedule where the loan amount actually increases through not paying the full interest
   - Amortized analysis, analyzing the execution cost of algorithms over a sequence of operations.
   - _____ of capital expenditures of certain assets under accounting rules, particularly intangible assets, in a manner analogous to depreciation.
   - _____

   a. Annuity
   b. Amortization
   c. Intangible
   d. EBIT

8. _____ are financial statements that factor the holding company's subsidiaries into its aggregated accounting figure. It is a representation of how the holding company is doing as a group. The consolidated accounts should provide a true and fair view of the financial and operating conditions of the group.
   a. Committee on Accounting Procedure
   b. Replacement cost
   c. Redemption value
   d. Consolidated financial statements

Chapter 3. Consolidated Financial Statements-Date of Acquisition,

9. The _____ of 1977 (15 U.S.C. §§ 78dd-1, et seq.) is a United States federal law known primarily for two of its main provisions, one that addresses accounting transparency requirements under the Securities Exchange Act of 1934 and another concerning bribery of foreign officials.

   a. Lease   b. Pre-emption right
   c. Competition law   d. Foreign Corrupt Practices Act

10. _____ was founded in June 1973 in London and replaced by the International Accounting Standards Board on April 1, 2001. It was responsible for developing the International Accounting Standards and promoting the use and application of these standards.

The _____ was founded as a result of an agreement between accountancy bodies in the following countries:

- Australia (Institute of Chartered Accountants in Australia (ICAA) and the CPA Australia (formerly known as Australian Society of Certified Practising Accountants (ASCPA))

- Canada (Canadian Institute of Chartered Accountants (CICA))

- France (Ordre des Experts Comptable et des Comptables Agrees (Order of Accounting Experts and Qualified Accountants))

- Germany and the Wirtschaftsprüferkammer (WPK) (Chamber of Auditors))

- Japan Nihon Kouninkaikeishi Kyoukai)

- Mexico (Instituto Mexicano de Contadores Publicos (IMCP) (Mexican Institute of Public Accountants)) (removed from the board in 1987 due to non-payment of dues; resumed in 1995.)

- the Netherlands (Nederlands Instituut van Registeraccountants (NIVRA)

(Netherlands Institute of Registered Auditors))

- the United Kingdom and Ireland (counted as one) (Institute of Chartered Accountants in England and Wales (ICAEW), Institute of Chartered Accountants of Scotland (ICAS), Institute of Chartered Accountants in Ireland (ICAI), Association of Certified Accountants, Institute of Cost and Management Accountants, and the Institute of Municipal Treasurers and Accountants)

- the United States of America (American Institute of Certified Public Accountants (AICPA))

The Institute of Chartered Accountants of Nigeria became an associate member in 1976 and a member of the board from 1978 to 1987.

The National Council of Chartered Accountants (South Africa) became an associate member in 1974 and joined the board in 1978.

a. American Payroll Association
c. American Accounting Association
b. International Accounting Standards Board
d. International Accounting Standards Committee

11. A _____ is a fungible, negotiable instrument representing financial value. they are broadly categorized into debt securities (such as banknotes, bonds and debentures), and equity securities; e.g., common stocks. The company or other entity issuing the _____ is called the issuer.
   a. 3M Company
   b. BMC Software, Inc.
   c. Tracking stock
   d. Security

12. The U.S. _____ is an independent agency of the United States government which holds primary responsibility for enforcing the federal securities laws and regulating the securities industry, the nation's stock and options exchanges, and other electronic securities markets. The SEC was created by section 4 of the Securities Exchange Act of 1934 (now codified as 15 U.S.C. ÂÂ§ 78d and commonly referred to as the 1934 Act.)
   a. BMC Software, Inc.
   b. Securities and Exchange Commission
   c. 3M Company
   d. BNSF Railway

13. _____ are formal records of a business' financial activities.

In British English, including United Kingdom company law, _____ are often referred to as accounts, although the term _____ is also used, particularly by accountants.

_____ provide an overview of a business' financial condition in both short and long term.

   a. 3M Company
   b. Statement of retained earnings
   c. Notes to the financial statements
   d. Financial statements

14. A _____ occurs when a financial sponsor acquires a controlling interest in a company's equity and where a significant percentage of the purchase price is financed through leverage (borrowing.) The assets of the acquired company are used as collateral for the borrowed capital, sometimes with assets of the acquiring company. The bonds or other paper issued for a _____ is commonly considered not to be investment grade because of the significant risks involved.
   a. BNSF Railway
   b. Leveraged buyout
   c. BMC Software, Inc.
   d. 3M Company

15. In an economy, production, consumption and exchange are carried out by two basic _____: the firm and the household.
   a. ABC Television Network
   b. AMEX
   c. AIG
   d. Economic units

16. _____, in accrual accounting, is any account where the asset or liability is not realized until a future date (accounting period), e.g. annuities, charges, taxes, income, etc. The _____ item may be carried, dependent on type of deferral, as either an asset or liability.
   a. Cash basis accounting
   b. Pro forma
   c. Payroll
   d. Deferred

17. _____ is an accounting concept, meaning a future tax liability or asset, resulting from temporary differences between book (accounting) value of assets and liabilities and their tax value, or timing differences between the recognition of gains and losses in financial statements and their recognition in a tax computation.

Temporary differences are differences between the carrying amount of an asset or liability recognised in the balance sheet and the amount attributed to that asset or liability for tax purposes (the tax base.)

a. Deficit
b. Tax refund
c. Deferred tax
d. Federal tax revenue by state

18. In financial accounting, a _____ or statement of financial position is a summary of a person's or organization's balances. Assets, liabilities and ownership equity are listed as of a specific date, such as the end of its financial year. A _____ is often described as a snapshot of a company's financial condition.

a. Statement of retained earnings
b. Financial statements
c. 3M Company
d. Balance sheet

19. In accounting, _____ or carrying value is the value of an asset according to its balance sheet account balance. For assets, the value is based on the original cost of the asset less any depreciation, amortization or impairment costs made against the asset. Traditionally, a company's _____ is its total assets minus intangible assets and liabilities.

a. Depreciation
b. Generally accepted accounting principles
c. Book value
d. Matching principle

20. In accounting/accountancy, _____ are journal entries usually made at the end of an accounting period to allocate income and expenditure to the period in which they actually occurred. The revenue recognition principle is the basis of making _____ that pertain to unearned and accrued revenues under accrual-basis accounting. They are sometimes called Balance Day adjustments because they are made on balance day.

a. Earnings before interest, taxes, depreciation and amortization
b. Accrued expense
c. Accrual
d. Adjusting entries

21. In economics, business, retail, and accounting, a _____ is the value of money that has been used up to produce something, and hence is not available for use anymore. In economics, a _____ is an alternative that is given up as a result of a decision. In business, the _____ may be one of acquisition, in which case the amount of money expended to acquire it is counted as _____.

a. Cost
b. Cost allocation
c. Prime cost
d. Cost of quality

22. _____ in business is an accounting concept that refers to ownership of a company (subsidiary) that is less than 50% of outstanding shares. _____ belongs to other investors and is reported on the consolidated balance sheet of the owning company to reflect the claim on assets belonging to other, non-controlling shareholders. Also, _____ is reported on the consolidated income statement as a share of profit belonging to minority shareholders.

a. Credit memo
b. Bankruptcy prediction
c. Subledger
d. Minority interest

Chapter 3. Consolidated Financial Statements-Date of Acquisition,

23. _____ is a specific term used in companies' financial reporting from the company-whole point of view. Because that use excludes the effects of changing ownership interest, an economic measure of _____ is necessary for financial analysis from the shareholders' point of view

_____ is defined by the Financial Accounting Standards Board, or FASB, as 'the change in equity [net assets] of a business enterprise during a period from transactions and other events and circumstances from nonowner sources. It includes all changes in equity during a period except those resulting from investments by owners and distributions to owners.'

_____ is the sum of net income and other items that must bypass the income statement because they have not been realized, including items like an unrealized holding gain or loss from available for sale securities and foreign currency translation gains or losses.

a. BNSF Railway
b. 3M Company
c. BMC Software, Inc.
d. Comprehensive income

24. The phrase _____, according to the Organization for Economic Co-operation and Development, refers to 'creative work undertaken on a systematic basis in order to increase the stock of knowledge, including knowledge of man, culture and society, and the use of this stock of knowledge to devise new applications [sic]'

New product design and development is more than often a crucial factor in the survival of a company. In an industry that is fast changing, firms must continually revise their design and range of products. This is necessary due to continuous technology change and development as well as other competitors and the changing preference of customers.

a. 3M Company
b. BMC Software, Inc.
c. BNSF Railway
d. Research and development

25. A _____ or reacquired stock is stock which is bought back by the issuing company, reducing the amount of outstanding stock on the open market ('open market' including insiders' holdings).

Stock repurchases are often used as a tax-efficient method to put cash into shareholders' hands, rather than pay dividends. Sometimes, companies do this when they feel that their stock is undervalued on the open market.

a. Treasury stock
b. Matching principle
c. Cost of goods sold
d. Net profit

Chapter 4. Consolidated Financial Statements After Acquisition

1. _____ in accounting is the process of treating equity investments, usually 20-50%, in associate companies. The investor keeps such equities as an asset. Proportional share of associate company's net income increases the investment, and proportional payment of dividends decreases it.
   a. Out-of-pocket
   b. AIG
   c. Equity method
   d. ABC Television Network

2. In economics, business, retail, and accounting, a _____ is the value of money that has been used up to produce something, and hence is not available for use anymore. In economics, a _____ is an alternative that is given up as a result of a decision. In business, the _____ may be one of acquisition, in which case the amount of money expended to acquire it is counted as _____.
   a. Cost of quality
   b. Prime cost
   c. Cost allocation
   d. Cost

3. _____ are payments made by a corporation to its shareholder members. It is the portion of corporate profits paid out to stockholders. When a corporation earns a profit or surplus, that money can be put to two uses: it can either be re-invested in the business (called retained earnings), or it can be paid to the shareholders as a dividend.
   a. Dividends
   b. Dividend payout ratio
   c. Dividend yield
   d. Dividend stripping

4. _____ is a payment of a dividend to stockholders that exceeds the company's retained earnings. Once retained earnings is depleted, capital accounts such as additional paid-in capital are decreased to make up for the remaining dividend to be paid to stockholders. When a _____ occurs, it is considered to be a return of investment instead of profits.
   a. Redemption value
   b. Trade name
   c. Liquidating dividend
   d. Fund accounting

5. _____ are financial statements that factor the holding company's subsidiaries into its aggregated accounting figure. It is a representation of how the holding company is doing as a group. The consolidated accounts should provide a true and fair view of the financial and operating conditions of the group.
   a. Redemption value
   b. Consolidated financial statements
   c. Committee on Accounting Procedure
   d. Replacement cost

6. An _____ is the buying of one company by another. An _____ may be friendly or hostile. In the former case, the companies cooperate in negotiations; in the latter case, the takeover target is unwilling to be bought or the target's board has no prior knowledge of the offer. _____ usually refers to a purchase of a smaller firm by a larger one. Sometimes, however, a smaller firm will acquire management control of a larger or longer established company and keep its name for the combined entity. This is known as a reverse takeover.
   a. AIG
   b. AMEX
   c. ABC Television Network
   d. Acquisition

7. _____ are formal records of a business' financial activities.

In British English, including United Kingdom company law, _____ are often referred to as accounts, although the term _____ is also used, particularly by accountants.

_____ provide an overview of a business' financial condition in both short and long term.

Chapter 4. Consolidated Financial Statements After Acquisition

a. Notes to the financial statements
b. 3M Company
c. Statement of retained earnings
d. Financial statements

8. _____ is equal to the income that a firm has after subtracting costs and expenses from the total revenue. _____ can be distributed among holders of common stock as a dividend or held by the firm as retained earnings.

The items deducted will typically include tax expense, financing expense (interest expense), and minority interest. Likewise, preferred stock dividends will be subtracted too, though they are not an expense.

a. Long-term liabilities
b. Generally accepted accounting principles
c. Matching principle
d. Net income

9. A _____ is a type of business entity in which partners (owners) share with each other the profits or losses of the business undertaking in which all have invested. _____s are often favored over corporations for taxation purposes, as the _____ structure does not generally incur a tax on profits before it is distributed to the partners (i.e. there is no dividend tax levied.) However, depending on the _____ structure and the jurisdiction in which it operates, owners of a _____ may be exposed to greater personal liability than they would as shareholders of a corporation.

a. Resource Conservation and Recovery Act
b. Partnership
c. National Information Infrastructure Protection Act
d. Corporate governance

10. _____ in a corporation means to have control of a large enough block of voting stock shares in a company such that no one stock holder or coalition of stock holders can successfully oppose a motion. In theory this normally means that _____ would be 50% of the voting shares plus one.

In practice, though, _____ can be far less than that, as it is rare that 100% of a company's voting shareholders actively vote.

a. Participating preferred stock
b. Public offering
c. Controlling interest
d. Preferred stock

11. _____ is a specific term used in companies' financial reporting from the company-whole point of view. Because that use excludes the effects of changing ownership interest, an economic measure of _____ is necessary for financial analysis from the shareholders' point of view

_____ is defined by the Financial Accounting Standards Board, or FASB, as 'the change in equity [net assets] of a business enterprise during a period from transactions and other events and circumstances from nonowner sources. It includes all changes in equity during a period except those resulting from investments by owners and distributions to owners.'

_____ is the sum of net income and other items that must bypass the income statement because they have not been realized, including items like an unrealized holding gain or loss from available for sale securities and foreign currency translation gains or losses.

a. BMC Software, Inc.
b. 3M Company
c. BNSF Railway
d. Comprehensive income

Chapter 4. Consolidated Financial Statements After Acquisition

12. _____ is a fee paid on borrowed assets. It is the price paid for the use of borrowed money, or, money earned by deposited funds. Assets that are sometimes lent with _____ include money, shares, consumer goods through hire purchase, major assets such as aircraft, and even entire factories in finance lease arrangements. The _____ is calculated upon the value of the assets in the same manner as upon money.

    a. ABC Television Network
    b. AIG
    c. Interest
    d. Insolvency

13. The _____ of 1977 (15 U.S.C. ÂÂ§ÂÂ§ 78dd-1, et seq.) is a United States federal law known primarily for two of its main provisions, one that addresses accounting transparency requirements under the Securities Exchange Act of 1934 and another concerning bribery of foreign officials.

    a. Competition law
    b. Lease
    c. Pre-emption right
    d. Foreign Corrupt Practices Act

14. A _____ is a fungible, negotiable instrument representing financial value. they are broadly categorized into debt securities (such as banknotes, bonds and debentures), and equity securities; e.g., common stocks. The company or other entity issuing the _____ is called the issuer.

    a. BMC Software, Inc.
    b. 3M Company
    c. Security
    d. Tracking stock

15. The U.S. _____ is an independent agency of the United States government which holds primary responsibility for enforcing the federal securities laws and regulating the securities industry, the nation's stock and options exchanges, and other electronic securities markets. The SEC was created by section 4 of the Securities Exchange Act of 1934 (now codified as 15 U.S.C. ÂÂ§ 78d and commonly referred to as the 1934 Act.)

    a. 3M Company
    b. BMC Software, Inc.
    c. BNSF Railway
    d. Securities and Exchange Commission

16. A _____, in business matters, is an entity that is controlled by a bigger and more powerful entity. The controlled entity is called a company, corporation, or limited liability company, and the controlling entity is called its parent (or the parent company.) The reason for this distinction is that a lone company cannot be a _____ of any organization; only an entity representing a legal fiction as a separate entity can be a _____.

    a. Parent company
    b. Subsidiary
    c. BMC Software, Inc.
    d. 3M Company

17. _____ is the balance of the amounts of cash being received and paid by a business during a defined period of time, sometimes tied to a specific project. Measurement of _____ can be used

    - to evaluate the state or performance of a business or project.
    - to determine problems with liquidity. Being profitable does not necessarily mean being liquid. A company can fail because of a shortage of cash, even while profitable.
    - to project rate of returns. The time of _____s into and out of projects are used as inputs to financial models such as internal rate of return, and net present value.
    - to examine income or growth of a business when it is believed that accrual accounting concepts do not represent economic realities. Alternately, _____ can be used to 'validate' the net income generated by accrual accounting.

Chapter 4. Consolidated Financial Statements After Acquisition

_____ as a generic term may be used differently depending on context, and certain _____ definitions may be adapted by analysts and users for their own uses. Common terms include operating _____ and free _____.

a. Commercial paper
b. Controlling interest
c. Cash flow
d. Flow-through entity

18. In financial accounting, a _____ or Statement of cash flows is a financial statement that shows a company's flow of cash. The money coming into the business is called cash inflow, and money going out from the business is called cash outflow. The statement shows how changes in balance sheet and income accounts affect cash and cash equivalents, and breaks the analysis down to operating, investing, and financing activities.

a. BMC Software, Inc.
b. BNSF Railway
c. 3M Company
d. Cash flow statement

19. _____, in accrual accounting, is any account where the asset or liability is not realized until a future date (accounting period), e.g. annuities, charges, taxes, income, etc. The _____ item may be carried, dependent on type of deferral, as either an asset or liability.

a. Payroll
b. Cash basis accounting
c. Pro forma
d. Deferred

20. _____ is an accounting concept, meaning a future tax liability or asset, resulting from temporary differences between book (accounting) value of assets and liabilities and their tax value, or timing differences between the recognition of gains and losses in financial statements and their recognition in a tax computation.

Temporary differences are differences between the carrying amount of an asset or liability recognised in the balance sheet and the amount attributed to that asset or liability for tax purposes (the tax base.)

a. Federal tax revenue by state
b. Deficit
c. Tax refund
d. Deferred tax

21. An _____ is a tax levied on the financial income of people, corporations, or other legal entities. Various _____ systems exist, with varying degrees of tax incidence. Income taxation can be progressive, proportional, or regressive.

a. Implied level of government service
b. Ordinary income
c. Individual Retirement Arrangement
d. Income tax

Chapter 5. Allocation and Depreciation of Differences Between Cost and Book Values

1. A _____ is the grant of authority or rights, stating that the granter formally recognizes the prerogative of the recipient to exercise the rights specified. It is implicit that the granter retains superiority (or sovereignty), and that the recipient admits a limited (or inferior) status within the relationship, and it is within that sense that _____s were historically granted, and that sense is retained in modern usage of the term. Also, _____ can simply be a document giving royal permission to start a colony.
   a. Scottish Poor Laws
   b. False Claims Act
   c. Charter
   d. Covenant

2. The _____ of 1977 (15 U.S.C. §§ 78dd-1, et seq.) is a United States federal law known primarily for two of its main provisions, one that addresses accounting transparency requirements under the Securities Exchange Act of 1934 and another concerning bribery of foreign officials.
   a. Lease
   b. Pre-emption right
   c. Competition law
   d. Foreign Corrupt Practices Act

3. A _____ is a fungible, negotiable instrument representing financial value. they are broadly categorized into debt securities (such as banknotes, bonds and debentures), and equity securities; e.g., common stocks. The company or other entity issuing the _____ is called the issuer.
   a. BMC Software, Inc.
   b. 3M Company
   c. Tracking stock
   d. Security

4. The U.S. _____ is an independent agency of the United States government which holds primary responsibility for enforcing the federal securities laws and regulating the securities industry, the nation's stock and options exchanges, and other electronic securities markets. The SEC was created by section 4 of the Securities Exchange Act of 1934 (now codified as 15 U.S.C. §§ 78d and commonly referred to as the 1934 Act.)
   a. 3M Company
   b. BNSF Railway
   c. BMC Software, Inc.
   d. Securities and Exchange Commission

5. A _____, in business matters, is an entity that is controlled by a bigger and more powerful entity. The controlled entity is called a company, corporation, or limited liability company, and the controlling entity is called its parent (or the parent company.) The reason for this distinction is that a lone company cannot be a _____ of any organization; only an entity representing a legal fiction as a separate entity can be a _____.
   a. 3M Company
   b. Parent company
   c. BMC Software, Inc.
   d. Subsidiary

6. In accounting, _____ or carrying value is the value of an asset according to its balance sheet account balance. For assets, the value is based on the original cost of the asset less any depreciation, amortization or impairment costs made against the asset. Traditionally, a company's _____ is its total assets minus intangible assets and liabilities.
   a. Generally accepted accounting principles
   b. Matching principle
   c. Depreciation
   d. Book value

7. In economics, business, retail, and accounting, a _____ is the value of money that has been used up to produce something, and hence is not available for use anymore. In economics, a _____ is an alternative that is given up as a result of a decision. In business, the _____ may be one of acquisition, in which case the amount of money expended to acquire it is counted as _____.
   a. Cost of quality
   b. Prime cost
   c. Cost allocation
   d. Cost

Chapter 5. Allocation and Depreciation of Differences Between Cost and Book Values 25

8. _____ is the process of increasing, or accounting for, an amount over a period of time. Particular instances of the term include:

- _____, the allocation of a lump sum amount to different time periods, particularly for loans and other forms of finance, including related interest or other finance charges.
    - _____ schedule, a table detailing each periodic payment on a loan (typically a mortgage), as generated by an _____ calculator.
    - Negative _____, an _____ schedule where the loan amount actually increases through not paying the full interest
- Amortized analysis, analyzing the execution cost of algorithms over a sequence of operations.
- _____ of capital expenditures of certain assets under accounting rules, particularly intangible assets, in a manner analogous to depreciation.
- _____

a. Amortization
c. Annuity
b. Intangible
d. EBIT

9. _____ is a term used in accounting, economics and finance to spread the cost of an asset over the span of several years.

In simple words we can say that _____ is the reduction in the value of an asset due to usage, passage of time, wear and tear, technological outdating or obsolescence, depletion, inadequacy, rot, rust, decay or other such factors.

In accounting, _____ is a term used to describe any method of attributing the historical or purchase cost of an asset across its useful life, roughly corresponding to normal wear and tear.

a. Current asset
c. Net profit
b. General ledger
d. Depreciation

10. In accounting, _____ has a very specific meaning. It is an outflow of cash or other valuable assets from a person or company to another person or company. This outflow of cash is generally one side of a trade for products or services that have equal or better current or future value to the buyer than to the seller.

a. ABC Television Network
c. AMEX
b. AIG
d. Expense

11. An _____ is the buying of one company by another. An _____ may be friendly or hostile. In the former case, the companies cooperate in negotiations; in the latter case, the takeover target is unwilling to be bought or the target's board has no prior knowledge of the offer. _____ usually refers to a purchase of a smaller firm by a larger one. Sometimes, however, a smaller firm will acquire management control of a larger or longer established company and keep its name for the combined entity. This is known as a reverse takeover.

a. AMEX
c. ABC Television Network
b. AIG
d. Acquisition

Chapter 5. Allocation and Depreciation of Differences Between Cost and Book Values

12. In business and accounting, _____ are everything of value that is owned by a person or company. It is a claim on the property your income of a borrower. The balance sheet of a firm records the monetary value of the _____ owned by the firm.

    a. Accounts receivable
    b. Accrual basis accounting
    c. Assets
    d. Earnings before interest, taxes, depreciation and amortization

13. _____, also called fair price (in a commonplace conflation of the two distinct concepts), is a concept used in finance and economics, defined as a rational and unbiased estimate of the potential market price of a good, service, or asset, taking into account such objective factors as:

- acquisition/production/distribution costs, replacement costs, or costs of close substitutes
- actual utility at a given level of development of social productive capability
- supply vs. demand

and subjective factors such as

- risk characteristics
- cost of capital
- individually perceived utility

In accounting, _____ is used as an estimate of the market value of an asset (or liability) for which a market price cannot be determined (usually because there is no established market for the asset.) Under GAAP (FAS 157), _____ is the amount at which the asset could be bought or sold in a current transaction between willing parties, or transferred to an equivalent party, other than in a liquidation sale. This is used for assets whose carrying value is based on mark-to-market valuations; for assets carried at historical cost, the _____ of the asset is not used. One example of where _____ is an issue is a College kitchen with a cost of $2 million which was built 5 years ago.

    a. 3M Company
    b. BNSF Railway
    c. BMC Software, Inc.
    d. Fair value

14. _____ are sometimes the same as net worth, or shareholders' equity - assets minus liabilities. The term _____ is commonly used with charities or not for profit entities. Although these entities don't make money, it is important to maintain reasonable reserves to help future growth.

    a. Net interest spread
    b. Debtor days
    c. Sortino ratio
    d. Net assets

15. _____ is equal to the income that a firm has after subtracting costs and expenses from the total revenue. _____ can be distributed among holders of common stock as a dividend or held by the firm as retained earnings.

The items deducted will typically include tax expense, financing expense (interest expense), and minority interest. Likewise, preferred stock dividends will be subtracted too, though they are not an expense.

Chapter 5. Allocation and Depreciation of Differences Between Cost and Book Values

a. Long-term liabilities
c. Matching principle
b. Generally accepted accounting principles
d. Net income

16. In financial accounting, _____ or cost of sales includes the direct costs attributable to the production of the goods sold by a company. This amount includes the materials cost used in creating the goods along with the direct labor costs used to produce the good. It excludes indirect expenses such as distribution costs and sales force costs.
   a. 3M Company
   c. FIFO and LIFO accounting
   b. Reorder point
   d. Cost of Goods Sold

17. _____ is a specific term used in companies' financial reporting from the company-whole point of view. Because that use excludes the effects of changing ownership interest, an economic measure of _____ is necessary for financial analysis from the shareholders' point of view

_____ is defined by the Financial Accounting Standards Board, or FASB, as 'the change in equity [net assets] of a business enterprise during a period from transactions and other events and circumstances from nonowner sources. It includes all changes in equity during a period except those resulting from investments by owners and distributions to owners.'

_____ is the sum of net income and other items that must bypass the income statement because they have not been realized, including items like an unrealized holding gain or loss from available for sale securities and foreign currency translation gains or losses.

   a. BMC Software, Inc.
   c. BNSF Railway
   b. 3M Company
   d. Comprehensive income

18. _____ is a fee paid on borrowed assets. It is the price paid for the use of borrowed money, or, money earned by deposited funds. Assets that are sometimes lent with _____ include money, shares, consumer goods through hire purchase, major assets such as aircraft, and even entire factories in finance lease arrangements. The _____ is calculated upon the value of the assets in the same manner as upon money.
   a. Interest
   c. Insolvency
   b. AIG
   d. ABC Television Network

19. _____ in accounting is the process of treating equity investments, usually 20-50%, in associate companies. The investor keeps such equities as an asset. Proportional share of associate company's net income increases the investment, and proportional payment of dividends decreases it.
   a. ABC Television Network
   c. Equity method
   b. Out-of-pocket
   d. AIG

20. _____ in a corporation means to have control of a large enough block of voting stock shares in a company such that no one stock holder or coalition of stock holders can successfully oppose a motion. In theory this normally means that _____ would be 50% of the voting shares plus one.

In practice, though, _____ can be far less than that, as it is rare that 100% of a company's voting shareholders actively vote.

Chapter 5. Allocation and Depreciation of Differences Between Cost and Book Values

a. Preferred stock
b. Controlling interest
c. Participating preferred stock
d. Public offering

21. _____ is that which is owed; usually referencing assets owed, but the term can also cover moral obligations and other interactions not requiring money. In the case of assets, _____ is a means of using future purchasing power in the present before a summation has been earned. Some companies and corporations use _____ as a part of their overall corporate finance strategy.

a. Lender
b. Debt
c. Loan
d. Debenture

22. In economics, _____ or _____ goods or real _____ refers to factors of production used to create goods or services that are not themselves significantly consumed (though they may depreciate) in the production process. _____ goods may be acquired with money or financial _____. In finance and accounting, _____ generally refers to financial wealth, especially that used to start or maintain a business.

a. Capital
b. Screening
c. Vyborg Appeal
d. Disclosure

23. _____ is any physical or virtual entity that is owned by an individual or jointly by a group of individuals. An owner of _____ has the right to consume, sell, rent, mortgage, transfer and exchange his or her _____. Important widely-recognized types of _____ include real _____, personal _____ (other physical possessions), and intellectual _____ (rights over artistic creations, inventions, etc.), although the latter is not always as widely recognized or enforced.

a. Fiduciary
b. Property
c. Primary authority
d. Disclosure requirement

24. _____ are financial statements that factor the holding company's subsidiaries into its aggregated accounting figure. It is a representation of how the holding company is doing as a group. The consolidated accounts should provide a true and fair view of the financial and operating conditions of the group.

a. Replacement cost
b. Committee on Accounting Procedure
c. Consolidated financial statements
d. Redemption value

25. _____ are formal records of a business' financial activities.

In British English, including United Kingdom company law, _____ are often referred to as accounts, although the term _____ is also used, particularly by accountants.

_____ provide an overview of a business' financial condition in both short and long term.

a. 3M Company
b. Notes to the financial statements
c. Statement of retained earnings
d. Financial statements

26. A _____ is the pinnacle activity involved in selling products or services in return for money or other compensation. It is an act of completion of a commercial activity.

A _____ is completed by the seller, the owner of the goods.

Chapter 5. Allocation and Depreciation of Differences Between Cost and Book Values

a. High yield stock
c. Sale
b. Tertiary sector of economy
d. Maturity

27. The _____ is the former authoritative body of the American Institute of Certified Public Accountants (AICPA.) It was created by the American Institute of Certified Public Accountants in 1959 and issued pronouncements on accounting principles until 1973, when it was replaced by the Financial Accounting Standards Board (FASB.)

The _____ was disbanded in the hopes that the smaller, fully-independent FASB could more effectively create accounting standards.

a. American Payroll Association
c. Accounting Principles Board
b. Institute of Management Accountants
d. International Federation of Accountants

28. _____ were published by Accounting Principles Board (APB.) The board was created by American Institute of Certified Public Accountants (AICPA) in 1959 and was replaced by Financial Accounting Standards Board (FASB) in 1973. Its mission was to develop an overall conceptual framework of US generally accepted accounting principles (US GAAP.)

a. Accounting Principles Board Opinions
c. ABC Television Network
b. AIG
d. AMEX

Chapter 6. Elimination of Unrealized Profit on Intercompany Sales of Inventory

1. _____ is a common concept in economics, and gives rise to derived concepts such as consumer debt. Generally _____ is defined by opposition to production. But the precise definition can vary because different schools of economists define production quite differently.
   - a. Consumption
   - b. Mitigating Control
   - c. Starving the beast
   - d. Yield

2. A _____ is the pinnacle activity involved in selling products or services in return for money or other compensation. It is an act of completion of a commercial activity.

   A _____ is completed by the seller, the owner of the goods.
   - a. Tertiary sector of economy
   - b. Sale
   - c. High yield stock
   - d. Maturity

3. A _____ is a type of business entity in which partners (owners) share with each other the profits or losses of the business undertaking in which all have invested. _____s are often favored over corporations for taxation purposes, as the _____ structure does not generally incur a tax on profits before it is distributed to the partners (i.e. there is no dividend tax levied.) However, depending on the _____ structure and the jurisdiction in which it operates, owners of a _____ may be exposed to greater personal liability than they would as shareholders of a corporation.
   - a. National Information Infrastructure Protection Act
   - b. Partnership
   - c. Resource Conservation and Recovery Act
   - d. Corporate governance

4. The _____ , which includes revisions that are sometimes called the Revised _____ , is a uniform act (similar to a model statute), proposed by the National Conference of Commissioners on Uniform State Laws ('NCCUSL') for the governance of business partnerships by U.S. States. Several versions of _____ have been promulgated by the NCCUSL, the earliest having been put forth in 1914, and the most recent in 1997.

   The NCCUSL's first revision of _____ was promulgated in 1992 and amended in 1993 and 1994.
   - a. ABC Television Network
   - b. AMEX
   - c. Uniform Partnership Act
   - d. AIG

5. _____ is generally understood in financial circles as the point at which revenue is recognized, typically through a transaction which involves the exchange of an asset, product, or service for cash or its equivalents.

   This approach gives the accounting division a strictly objective basis for changing the books. For example, a homeowner may believe that his house has grown in value during a strong market, or fallen in value during a weak market, but until the house is actually sold for a specific price to a specific buyer, the change in value can only be estimated and is considered unrealized.
   - a. Total-factor productivity
   - b. Merck ' Co., Inc.
   - c. Valuation
   - d. Realization

6. In economics, business, retail, and accounting, a _____ is the value of money that has been used up to produce something, and hence is not available for use anymore. In economics, a _____ is an alternative that is given up as a result of a decision. In business, the _____ may be one of acquisition, in which case the amount of money expended to acquire it is counted as _____.

Chapter 6. Elimination of Unrealized Profit on Intercompany Sales of Inventory

a. Cost
b. Cost of quality
c. Prime cost
d. Cost allocation

7. In financial accounting, _____ or cost of sales includes the direct costs attributable to the production of the goods sold by a company. This amount includes the materials cost used in creating the goods along with the direct labor costs used to produce the good. It excludes indirect expenses such as distribution costs and sales force costs.

a. 3M Company
b. FIFO and LIFO accounting
c. Reorder point
d. Cost of goods sold

8. In accounting, _____ or sales profit is the difference between revenue and the cost of making a product or providing a service, before deducting overhead, payroll, taxation, and interest payments. Note that this is different from operating profit (earnings before interest and taxes.)

Net sales are calculated:

Net sales = Sales - Sales returns and allowances.

a. Participating preferred stock
b. Commercial paper
c. Capital structure
d. Gross profit

9. _____ is equal to the income that a firm has after subtracting costs and expenses from the total revenue. _____ can be distributed among holders of common stock as a dividend or held by the firm as retained earnings.

The items deducted will typically include tax expense, financing expense (interest expense), and minority interest. Likewise, preferred stock dividends will be subtracted too, though they are not an expense.

a. Long-term liabilities
b. Generally accepted accounting principles
c. Net income
d. Matching principle

10. _____ is a specific term used in companies' financial reporting from the company-whole point of view. Because that use excludes the effects of changing ownership interest, an economic measure of _____ is necessary for financial analysis from the shareholders' point of view

_____ is defined by the Financial Accounting Standards Board, or FASB, as 'the change in equity [net assets] of a business enterprise during a period from transactions and other events and circumstances from nonowner sources. It includes all changes in equity during a period except those resulting from investments by owners and distributions to owners.'

_____ is the sum of net income and other items that must bypass the income statement because they have not been realized, including items like an unrealized holding gain or loss from available for sale securities and foreign currency translation gains or losses.

a. BNSF Railway
b. BMC Software, Inc.
c. 3M Company
d. Comprehensive income

Chapter 6. Elimination of Unrealized Profit on Intercompany Sales of Inventory

11. _____ in accounting is the process of treating equity investments, usually 20-50%, in associate companies. The investor keeps such equities as an asset. Proportional share of associate company's net income increases the investment, and proportional payment of dividends decreases it.
    a. ABC Television Network
    b. AIG
    c. Out-of-pocket
    d. Equity method

12. _____, in accrual accounting, is any account where the asset or liability is not realized until a future date (accounting period), e.g. annuities, charges, taxes, income, etc. The _____ item may be carried, dependent on type of deferral, as either an asset or liability.
    a. Payroll
    b. Deferred
    c. Cash basis accounting
    d. Pro forma

13. _____ is an accounting concept, meaning a future tax liability or asset, resulting from temporary differences between book (accounting) value of assets and liabilities and their tax value, or timing differences between the recognition of gains and losses in financial statements and their recognition in a tax computation.

    Temporary differences are differences between the carrying amount of an asset or liability recognised in the balance sheet and the amount attributed to that asset or liability for tax purposes (the tax base.)

    a. Deficit
    b. Federal tax revenue by state
    c. Tax refund
    d. Deferred tax

14. _____ refers to a business or organization attempting to acquire goods or services to accomplish the goals of the enterprise. Though there are several organizations that attempt to set standards in the _____ process, processes can vary greatly between organizations. Typically the word e;_____ e; is not used interchangeably with the word e;procuremente;, since procurement typically includes Expediting, Supplier Quality, and Traffic and Logistics (T'L) in addition to _____.
    a. Consignor
    b. Free port
    c. Supply chain
    d. Purchasing

Chapter 7. Elimination of Unrealized Gains or Losses on Intercompany Sales

1. _____ is any physical or virtual entity that is owned by an individual or jointly by a group of individuals. An owner of _____ has the right to consume, sell, rent, mortgage, transfer and exchange his or her _____. Important widely-recognized types of _____ include real _____, personal _____ (other physical possessions), and intellectual _____ (rights over artistic creations, inventions, etc.), although the latter is not always as widely recognized or enforced.

   a. Disclosure requirement
   b. Property
   c. Fiduciary
   d. Primary authority

2. A _____ is the pinnacle activity involved in selling products or services in return for money or other compensation. It is an act of completion of a commercial activity.

   A _____ is completed by the seller, the owner of the goods.

   a. High yield stock
   b. Maturity
   c. Tertiary sector of economy
   d. Sale

3. _____ is generally understood in financial circles as the point at which revenue is recognized, typically through a transaction which involves the exchange of an asset, product, or service for cash or its equivalents.

   This approach gives the accounting division a strictly objective basis for changing the books. For example, a homeowner may believe that his house has grown in value during a strong market, or fallen in value during a weak market, but until the house is actually sold for a specific price to a specific buyer, the change in value can only be estimated and is considered unrealized.

   a. Realization
   b. Total-factor productivity
   c. Merck ' Co., Inc.
   d. Valuation

4. _____ is a fee paid on borrowed assets. It is the price paid for the use of borrowed money, or, money earned by deposited funds. Assets that are sometimes lent with _____ include money, shares, consumer goods through hire purchase, major assets such as aircraft, and even entire factories in finance lease arrangements. The _____ is calculated upon the value of the assets in the same manner as upon money.

   a. Interest
   b. AIG
   c. Insolvency
   d. ABC Television Network

5. _____ is a specific term used in companies' financial reporting from the company-whole point of view. Because that use excludes the effects of changing ownership interest, an economic measure of _____ is necessary for financial analysis from the shareholders' point of view

   _____ is defined by the Financial Accounting Standards Board, or FASB, as 'the change in equity [net assets] of a business enterprise during a period from transactions and other events and circumstances from nonowner sources. It includes all changes in equity during a period except those resulting from investments by owners and distributions to owners.'

   _____ is the sum of net income and other items that must bypass the income statement because they have not been realized, including items like an unrealized holding gain or loss from available for sale securities and foreign currency translation gains or losses.

Chapter 7. Elimination of Unrealized Gains or Losses on Intercompany Sales

    a. BMC Software, Inc.
    b. 3M Company
    c. BNSF Railway
    d. Comprehensive income

6. In economics, business, retail, and accounting, a _____ is the value of money that has been used up to produce something, and hence is not available for use anymore. In economics, a _____ is an alternative that is given up as a result of a decision. In business, the _____ may be one of acquisition, in which case the amount of money expended to acquire it is counted as _____.
    a. Cost of quality
    b. Cost allocation
    c. Prime cost
    d. Cost

7. _____ in accounting is the process of treating equity investments, usually 20-50%, in associate companies. The investor keeps such equities as an asset. Proportional share of associate company's net income increases the investment, and proportional payment of dividends decreases it.
    a. Equity method
    b. ABC Television Network
    c. Out-of-pocket
    d. AIG

8. _____ refers to a business or organization attempting to acquire goods or services to accomplish the goals of the enterprise. Though there are several organizations that attempt to set standards in the _____ process, processes can vary greatly between organizations. Typically the word e;_____e; is not used interchangeably with the word e;procuremente;, since procurement typically includes Expediting, Supplier Quality, and Traffic and Logistics (T'L) in addition to _____.
    a. Consignor
    b. Free port
    c. Supply chain
    d. Purchasing

9. _____ is equal to the income that a firm has after subtracting costs and expenses from the total revenue. _____ can be distributed among holders of common stock as a dividend or held by the firm as retained earnings.

The items deducted will typically include tax expense, financing expense (interest expense), and minority interest. Likewise, preferred stock dividends will be subtracted too, though they are not an expense.

    a. Long-term liabilities
    b. Generally accepted accounting principles
    c. Net income
    d. Matching principle

10. _____, in accrual accounting, is any account where the asset or liability is not realized until a future date (accounting period), e.g. annuities, charges, taxes, income, etc. The _____ item may be carried, dependent on type of deferral, as either an asset or liability.
    a. Deferred
    b. Cash basis accounting
    c. Pro forma
    d. Payroll

11. _____ is an accounting concept, meaning a future tax liability or asset, resulting from temporary differences between book (accounting) value of assets and liabilities and their tax value, or timing differences between the recognition of gains and losses in financial statements and their recognition in a tax computation.

Temporary differences are differences between the carrying amount of an asset or liability recognised in the balance sheet and the amount attributed to that asset or liability for tax purposes (the tax base.)

a. Federal tax revenue by state
c. Deficit

b. Tax refund
d. Deferred tax

Chapter 8. Changes in Ownership Interest

1. _____ is the state or fact of exclusive rights and control over property, which may be an object, land/real estate or intellectual property. An _____ right is also referred to as title.

   _____ is the key building block in the development of the capitalist socio-economic system.

   a. Encumbrance
   b. Ownership
   c. ABC Television Network
   d. Administrative proceeding

2. _____ is a fee paid on borrowed assets. It is the price paid for the use of borrowed money, or, money earned by deposited funds. Assets that are sometimes lent with _____ include money, shares, consumer goods through hire purchase, major assets such as aircraft, and even entire factories in finance lease arrangements. The _____ is calculated upon the value of the assets in the same manner as upon money.
   a. ABC Television Network
   b. Insolvency
   c. AIG
   d. Interest

3. In economics, business, retail, and accounting, a _____ is the value of money that has been used up to produce something, and hence is not available for use anymore. In economics, a _____ is an alternative that is given up as a result of a decision. In business, the _____ may be one of acquisition, in which case the amount of money expended to acquire it is counted as _____.
   a. Prime cost
   b. Cost of quality
   c. Cost allocation
   d. Cost

4. An _____ is the buying of one company by another. An _____ may be friendly or hostile. In the former case, the companies cooperate in negotiations; in the latter case, the takeover target is unwilling to be bought or the target's board has no prior knowledge of the offer. _____ usually refers to a purchase of a smaller firm by a larger one. Sometimes, however, a smaller firm will acquire management control of a larger or longer established company and keep its name for the combined entity. This is known as a reverse takeover.
   a. ABC Television Network
   b. AMEX
   c. AIG
   d. Acquisition

5. A _____ is the pinnacle activity involved in selling products or services in return for money or other compensation. It is an act of completion of a commercial activity.

   A _____ is completed by the seller, the owner of the goods.

   a. Tertiary sector of economy
   b. Maturity
   c. High yield stock
   d. Sale

6. A _____, in business matters, is an entity that is controlled by a bigger and more powerful entity. The controlled entity is called a company, corporation, or limited liability company, and the controlling entity is called its parent (or the parent company.) The reason for this distinction is that a lone company cannot be a _____ of any organization; only an entity representing a legal fiction as a separate entity can be a _____.
   a. BMC Software, Inc.
   b. 3M Company
   c. Parent company
   d. Subsidiary

7. A _____ or reacquired stock is stock which is bought back by the issuing company, reducing the amount of outstanding stock on the open market ('open market' including insiders' holdings).

Chapter 8. Changes in Ownership Interest

Stock repurchases are often used as a tax-efficient method to put cash into shareholders' hands, rather than pay dividends. Sometimes, companies do this when they feel that their stock is undervalued on the open market.

- a. Net profit
- b. Matching principle
- c. Cost of goods sold
- d. Treasury stock

8. _____ in accounting is the process of treating equity investments, usually 20-50%, in associate companies. The investor keeps such equities as an asset. Proportional share of associate company's net income increases the investment, and proportional payment of dividends decreases it.
   - a. ABC Television Network
   - b. Out-of-pocket
   - c. AIG
   - d. Equity method

9. In management accounting, _____ establishes budget and actual cost of operations, processes, departments or product and the analysis of variances, profitability or social use of funds. Managers use _____ to support decision-making to cut a company's costs and improve profitability. As a form of management accounting, _____ need not follow standards such as GAAP, because its primary use is for internal managers, rather than outside users, and what to compute is instead decided pragmatically.
   - a. Cost-volume-profit analysis
   - b. Marginal cost
   - c. Prime cost
   - d. Cost Accounting

Chapter 9. Intercompany Bond Holdings and Miscellaneous Topics

1. In finance, a _____ is a debt security, in which the authorized issuer owes the holders a debt and, depending on the terms of the _____, is obliged to pay interest (the coupon) and/or to repay the principal at a later date, termed maturity. It is a formal contract to repay borrowed money with interest at fixed intervals.

   Thus a _____ is like a loan: the issuer is the borrower, the _____ holder is the lender, and the coupon is the interest.

   a. Coupon rate
   c. Revenue bonds
   b. Zero-coupon bond
   d. Bond

2. An _____ is the buying of one company by another. An _____ may be friendly or hostile. In the former case, the companies cooperate in negotiations; in the latter case, the takeover target is unwilling to be bought or the target's board has no prior knowledge of the offer. _____ usually refers to a purchase of a smaller firm by a larger one. Sometimes, however, a smaller firm will acquire management control of a larger or longer established company and keep its name for the combined entity. This is known as a reverse takeover.

   a. AIG
   c. AMEX
   b. ABC Television Network
   d. Acquisition

3. _____ in accounting is the process of treating equity investments, usually 20-50%, in associate companies. The investor keeps such equities as an asset. Proportional share of associate company's net income increases the investment, and proportional payment of dividends decreases it.

   a. Equity method
   c. Out-of-pocket
   b. AIG
   d. ABC Television Network

4. In economics, business, retail, and accounting, a _____ is the value of money that has been used up to produce something, and hence is not available for use anymore. In economics, a _____ is an alternative that is given up as a result of a decision. In business, the _____ may be one of acquisition, in which case the amount of money expended to acquire it is counted as _____.

   a. Cost of quality
   c. Prime cost
   b. Cost
   d. Cost allocation

5. _____ represents claims for which formal instruments of credit are issued as evidence of debt, such as a promissory note. The credit instrument normally requires the debtor to pay interest and extends for time periods of 60-90 days or longer.

   a. Moving average
   c. Restricted stock
   b. Public offering
   d. Notes receivable

6. _____ are payments made by a corporation to its shareholder members. It is the portion of corporate profits paid out to stockholders. When a corporation earns a profit or surplus, that money can be put to two uses: it can either be re-invested in the business (called retained earnings), or it can be paid to the shareholders as a dividend.

   a. Dividend stripping
   c. Dividends
   b. Dividend payout ratio
   d. Dividend yield

7. A _____, in business matters, is an entity that is controlled by a bigger and more powerful entity. The controlled entity is called a company, corporation, or limited liability company, and the controlling entity is called its parent (or the parent company.) The reason for this distinction is that a lone company cannot be a _____ of any organization; only an entity representing a legal fiction as a separate entity can be a _____.

Chapter 9. Intercompany Bond Holdings and Miscellaneous Topics

    a. Parent company
    b. 3M Company
    c. Subsidiary
    d. BMC Software, Inc.

8. _____ is a specific term used in companies' financial reporting from the company-whole point of view. Because that use excludes the effects of changing ownership interest, an economic measure of _____ is necessary for financial analysis from the shareholders' point of view

_____ is defined by the Financial Accounting Standards Board, or FASB, as 'the change in equity [net assets] of a business enterprise during a period from transactions and other events and circumstances from nonowner sources. It includes all changes in equity during a period except those resulting from investments by owners and distributions to owners.'

_____ is the sum of net income and other items that must bypass the income statement because they have not been realized, including items like an unrealized holding gain or loss from available for sale securities and foreign currency translation gains or losses.

    a. BNSF Railway
    b. BMC Software, Inc.
    c. 3M Company
    d. Comprehensive income

9. _____ is typically a 'higher ranking' stock than voting shares, and its terms are negotiated between the corporation and the investor.

_____ usually carries no voting rights, but may carry superior priority over common stock in the payment of dividends and upon liquidation. _____ may carry a dividend that is paid out prior to any dividends being paid to common stock holders.

    a. Restricted stock
    b. Preferred stock
    c. Cash flow
    d. Gross income

10. _____ is a form of corporation equity ownership represented in the securities. It is a stock whose dividends are based on market fluctuations. It is dangerous in comparison to preferred shares and some other investment options, in that in the event of bankruptcy, _____ investors receive their funds after preferred stock holders, bondholders, creditors, etc. On the other hand, common shares on average perform better than preferred shares or bonds over time.

    a. 3M Company
    b. Stock split
    c. Common Stock
    d. Growth investing

11. _____ is a fee paid on borrowed assets. It is the price paid for the use of borrowed money , or, money earned by deposited funds .Assets that are sometimes lent with _____ include money, shares, consumer goods through hire purchase, major assets such as aircraft, and even entire factories in finance lease arrangements. The _____ is calculated upon the value of the assets in the same manner as upon money.

    a. Insolvency
    b. ABC Television Network
    c. Interest
    d. AIG

12. _____ in economics and business is the result of an exchange and from that trade we assign a numerical monetary value to a good, service or asset. If Alice trades Bob 4 apples for an orange, the _____ of an orange is 4 apples. Inversely, the _____ of an apple is 1/4 oranges.

a. Price discrimination
b. Discounts and allowances
c. Transactional Net Margin Method
d. Price

13. A mutual shareholder or _____ is an individual or company (including a corporation) that legally owns one or more shares of stock in a joint stock company. A company's shareholders collectively own that company. Thus, the typical goal of such companies is to enhance shareholder value.
   a. 3M Company
   b. Stock split
   c. Growth investing
   d. Stockholder

14. In accounting, _____ or carrying value is the value of an asset according to its balance sheet account balance. For assets, the value is based on the original cost of the asset less any depreciation, amortization or impairment costs made against the asset. Traditionally, a company's _____ is its total assets minus intangible assets and liabilities.
   a. Matching principle
   b. Book value
   c. Generally accepted accounting principles
   d. Depreciation

Chapter 10. Insolvency—Liquidation and Reorganization

1. _____ is a legally declared inability or impairment of ability of an individual or organization to pay its creditors. Creditors may file a _____ petition against a debtor ('involuntary _____') in an effort to recoup a portion of what they are owed or initiate a restructuring. In the majority of cases, however, _____ is initiated by the debtor (a 'voluntary _____' that is filed by the bankrupt individual or organization.)
   a. Bankruptcy
   b. BMC Software, Inc.
   c. Bankruptcy protection
   d. 3M Company

2. _____ means the inability to pay one's debts as they fall due. Usually used in Business terms, _____ refers to the inability for a 'limited liability' company to pay off debts.

   This is defined in two different ways:

   Cash flow _____ -
       Unable to pay debts as they fall due.

   a. Interest
   b. Insolvency
   c. ABC Television Network
   d. AIG

3. A _____ is a party (e.g. person, organization, company, or government) that has a claim to the services of a second party. It is a person or institution to whom money is owed. The first party, in general, has provided some property or service to the second party under the assumption (usually enforced by contract) that the second party will return an equivalent property or service.
   a. Treasury company
   b. Payback period
   c. Par value
   d. Creditor

4. _____ are sometimes the same as net worth, or shareholders' equity - assets minus liabilities. The term _____ is commonly used with charities or not for profit entities. Although these entities don't make money, it is important to maintain reasonable reserves to help future growth.
   a. Debtor days
   b. Sortino ratio
   c. Net assets
   d. Net interest spread

5. In business and accounting, _____ are everything of value that is owned by a person or company. It is a claim on the property your income of a borrower. The balance sheet of a firm records the monetary value of the _____ owned by the firm.
   a. Earnings before interest, taxes, depreciation and amortization
   b. Accrual basis accounting
   c. Accounts receivable
   d. Assets

6. In economics a _____ is an entity that owes a debt to someone else. The entity may be an individual, a firm, a government, a company or other legal person. The counterparty is called a creditor.
   a. Segregated portfolio company
   b. Fair market value
   c. Shares authorized
   d. Debtor

7. Procedural law comprises the rule by which a court hears and determines what happens in civil lawsuit or criminal _____. The rules are designed to ensure a fair and consistent application of due process (in the U.S.) or fundamental justice (in other common law countries) to all cases that come before a court.

a. Proceedings	b. Hospital Survey and Construction Act
c. Lease	d. Pre-emption right

8. The U.S. _____ is an independent agency of the United States government which holds primary responsibility for enforcing the federal securities laws and regulating the securities industry, the nation's stock and options exchanges, and other electronic securities markets. The SEC was created by section 4 of the Securities Exchange Act of 1934 (now codified as 15 U.S.C. ÂÂ§ 78d and commonly referred to as the 1934 Act.)

a. Securities and Exchange Commission	b. BNSF Railway
c. 3M Company	d. BMC Software, Inc.

9. In law, _____ refers to the process by which a company (or part of a company) is brought to an end, and the assets and property of the company redistributed. _____ can also be referred to as winding-up or dissolution, although dissolution technically refers to the last stage of _____. The process of _____ also arises when customs, an authority or agency in a country responsible for collecting and safeguarding customs duties, determines the final computation or ascertainment of the duties or drawback accruing on an entry.

a. Bankruptcy protection	b. BMC Software, Inc.
c. 3M Company	d. Liquidation

10. _____ is a legal term that refers to a holder of property on behalf of a beneficiary. A trust can be set up either to benefit particular persons, or for any charitable purposes (but not generally for non-charitable purposes): typical examples are a will trust for the testator's children and family, a pension trust (to confer benefits on employees and their families), and a charitable trust. In all cases, the _____ may be a person or company, whether or not they are a prospective beneficiary.

a. Trustee	b. Cash cow
c. Performance measurement	d. Management by exception

11. An _____ is a practitioner of accountancy, which is the measurement, disclosure or provision of assurance about financial information that helps managers, investors, tax authorities and other decision makers make resource allocation decisions.

The word '_____' is derived from the French 'Compter' which took its origin from the Latin 'Computare'. The word was formerly written in English as 'Accomptant', but in process of time the word, which was always pronounced by dropping the 'p', became gradually changed both in pronunciation and in orthography to its present form.

a. AMEX	b. AIG
c. ABC Television Network	d. Accountant

12. _____ were documents issued by the Committee on Accounting Procedure between 1938 and 1959 on various accounting problems. They were discontinued with the dissolution of the Committee in 1959 under a recommendation from the Special Committee on Research Program. In all, 51 bulletins were issued, however, the lack of binding authority over AICPA's membership reduced the influence of, and compliance with the content of the bulletins.

a. AIG	b. ABC Television Network
c. Other postemployment benefits	d. Accounting Research Bulletins

Chapter 10. Insolvency—Liquidation and Reorganization 43

13. The _____ is the national, professional association of CPAs in the United States, with more than 330,000 members, including CPAs in business and industry, public practice, government, and education; student affiliates; and international associates. It sets ethical standards for the profession and U.S. auditing standards for audits of private companies; federal, state and local governments; and non-profit organizations.

Approximately 40% of its members are engaged in the practice of public accounting, in areas such as auditing, accounting, taxation, general business consulting, business valuation, personal financial planning and business technology.

  a. ABC Television Network
  b. Other postemployment benefits
  c. American Institute of Certified Public Accountants
  d. AIG

14. _____ is the statutory title of qualified accountants in the United States who have passed the Uniform _____ Examination and have met additional state education and experience requirements for certification as a _____. Individuals who have passed the Exam but have not either accomplished the required on-the-job experience or have previously met it but in the meantime have lapsed their continuing professional education are, in many states, permitted the designation '_____ Inactive' or an equivalent phrase. In most U.S. states, only _____s who are licensed are able to provide to the public attestation (including auditing) opinions on financial statements.

  a. Chartered Certified Accountant
  b. Chartered Accountant
  c. Certified Public Accountant
  d. Certified General Accountant

15. In accounting, _____ or carrying value is the value of an asset according to its balance sheet account balance. For assets, the value is based on the original cost of the asset less any depreciation, amortization or impairment costs made against the asset. Traditionally, a company's _____ is its total assets minus intangible assets and liabilities.

  a. Matching principle
  b. Book value
  c. Depreciation
  d. Generally accepted accounting principles

16. _____, also called fair price (in a commonplace conflation of the two distinct concepts), is a concept used in finance and economics, defined as a rational and unbiased estimate of the potential market price of a good, service, or asset, taking into account such objective factors as:

- acquisition/production/distribution costs, replacement costs, or costs of close substitutes
- actual utility at a given level of development of social productive capability
- supply vs. demand

and subjective factors such as

- risk characteristics
- cost of capital
- individually perceived utility

In accounting, _____ is used as an estimate of the market value of an asset (or liability) for which a market price cannot be determined (usually because there is no established market for the asset.) Under GAAP (FAS 157), _____ is the amount at which the asset could be bought or sold in a current transaction between willing parties, or transferred to an equivalent party, other than in a liquidation sale. This is used for assets whose carrying value is based on mark-to-market valuations; for assets carried at historical cost, the _____ of the asset is not used. One example of where _____ is an issue is a College kitchen with a cost of $2 million which was built 5 years ago.

a. BMC Software, Inc.
b. Fair value
c. 3M Company
d. BNSF Railway

17. The _____ is located in Norwalk, Connecticut. It is an independent, organization in the private sector that is responsible for oversight of the Financial Accounting Standards Board (FASB), the Governmental Accounting Standards Board (GASB), and their respective advisory councils.

a. 3M Company
b. BMC Software, Inc.
c. BNSF Railway
d. Financial Accounting Foundation

18. _____ is that which is owed; usually referencing assets owed, but the term can also cover moral obligations and other interactions not requiring money. In the case of assets, _____ is a means of using future purchasing power in the present before a summation has been earned. Some companies and corporations use _____ as a part of their overall corporate finance strategy.

a. Debenture
b. Debt
c. Loan
d. Lender

19. _____ is the corporate management term for the act of partially dismantling or otherwise reorganizing a company for the purpose of making it more profitable. Also known as corporate _____, debt _____ and financial _____.

_____ is often done as part of a bankruptcy or of a strategic takeover by another firm, such as a leveraged buyout by a private equity firm.

a. Net worth
b. Payback period
c. Fair market value
d. Restructuring

20. _____ is generally understood in financial circles as the point at which revenue is recognized, typically through a transaction which involves the exchange of an asset, product, or service for cash or its equivalents.

This approach gives the accounting division a strictly objective basis for changing the books. For example, a homeowner may believe that his house has grown in value during a strong market, or fallen in value during a weak market, but until the house is actually sold for a specific price to a specific buyer, the change in value can only be estimated and is considered unrealized.

a. Valuation
b. Merck ' Co., Inc.
c. Total-factor productivity
d. Realization

21. In financial accounting, a _____ is defined as an obligation of an entity arising from past transactions or events, the settlement of which may result in the transfer or use of assets, provision of services or other yielding of economic benefits in the future.
   a. Corporate governance
   b. False Claims Act
   c. Liability
   d. Vested

Chapter 11. International Accounting and the Global Economy

1. _____ is a fee paid on borrowed assets. It is the price paid for the use of borrowed money, or, money earned by deposited funds. Assets that are sometimes lent with _____ include money, shares, consumer goods through hire purchase, major assets such as aircraft, and even entire factories in finance lease arrangements. The _____ is calculated upon the value of the assets in the same manner as upon money.
   a. AIG
   b. Insolvency
   c. ABC Television Network
   d. Interest

2. In finance, the _____ between two currencies specifies how much one currency is worth in terms of the other. It is the value of a foreign nation's currency in terms of the home nation's currency. For example an _____ of 102 Japanese yen to the United States dollar means that JPY 102 is worth the same as USD 1.
   a. AMEX
   b. AIG
   c. ABC Television Network
   d. Exchange rate

3. _____ is an equity (stock) exchange located at 11 Wall Street in lower Manhattan, New York, USA.) It is the largest stock exchange in the world by dollar value of its listed companies' securities. As of October 2008, the combined capitalization of all domestic _____ listed companies was US$10.1 trillion.
   a. 3M Company
   b. BMC Software, Inc.
   c. BNSF Railway
   d. New York Stock Exchange

4. A _____, (formerly a securities exchange) is a corporation or mutual organization which provides 'trading' facilities for stock brokers and traders, to trade stocks and other securities. _____s also provide facilities for the issue and redemption of securities as well as other financial instruments and capital events including the payment of income and dividends. The securities traded on a _____ include: shares issued by companies, unit trusts, derivatives, pooled investment products and bonds.
   a. BNSF Railway
   b. 3M Company
   c. BMC Software, Inc.
   d. Stock Exchange

5. In monetary economics _____ can refer either to a particular _____, for example British Pounds or United States Dollars, or, to the coins and banknotes of a particular _____, which actually form only a small part of the monetary base of a nation's money supply. The other part of a nation's money supply consists of money deposited in banks (sometimes called deposit money), ownership of which can be transferred by means of checks (cheques in the United Kingdom and Australia) or other forms of money transfer such as credit and debit cards. Deposit money and _____ are 'money' in the sense that both are acceptable as a means of exchange, but money need not necessarily be '_____'.
   a. BMC Software, Inc.
   b. BNSF Railway
   c. 3M Company
   d. Currency

6. The _____ founded on April 1, 2001 is the successor of the International Accounting Standards Committee (IASC) founded in June 1973 in London. It is responsible for developing the International Financial Reporting Standards (new name for the International Accounting Standards issued after 2001), and promoting the use and application of these standards.

The _____ is an independent, privately-funded accounting standard-setter based in London, UK.

   a. International Accounting Standards Board
   b. Emerging technologies
   c. Institute of Management Accountants
   d. Information Systems Audit and Control Association

Chapter 11. International Accounting and the Global Economy

7. _____ was founded in June 1973 in London and replaced by the International Accounting Standards Board on April 1, 2001. It was responsible for developing the International Accounting Standards and promoting the use and application of these standards.

The _____ was founded as a result of an agreement between accountancy bodies in the following countries:

- Australia (Institute of Chartered Accountants in Australia (ICAA) and the CPA Australia (formerly known as Australian Society of Certified Practising Accountants (ASCPA))

- Canada (Canadian Institute of Chartered Accountants (CICA))

- France (Ordre des Experts Comptable et des Comptables Agrees (Order of Accounting Experts and Qualified Accountants))

- Germany and the Wirtschaftsprüferkammer (WPK) (Chamber of Auditors))

- Japan Nihon Kouninkaikeishi Kyoukai)

- Mexico (Instituto Mexicano de Contadores Publicos (IMCP) (Mexican Institute of Public Accountants)) (removed from the board in 1987 due to non-payment of dues; resumed in 1995.)

- the Netherlands (Nederlands Instituut van Registeraccountants (NIVRA)

(Netherlands Institute of Registered Auditors))

- the United Kingdom and Ireland (counted as one) (Institute of Chartered Accountants in England and Wales (ICAEW), Institute of Chartered Accountants of Scotland (ICAS), Institute of Chartered Accountants in Ireland (ICAI), Association of Certified Accountants, Institute of Cost and Management Accountants, and the Institute of Municipal Treasurers and Accountants)

- the United States of America (American Institute of Certified Public Accountants (AICPA))

The Institute of Chartered Accountants of Nigeria became an associate member in 1976 and a member of the board from 1978 to 1987.

The National Council of Chartered Accountants (South Africa) became an associate member in 1974 and joined the board in 1978.

a. International Accounting Standards Committee
b. American Payroll Association
c. International Accounting Standards Board
d. American Accounting Association

8. _____ is the term used to refer to the standard framework of guidelines for financial accounting used in any given jurisdiction. _____ includes the standards, conventions, and rules accountants follow in recording and summarizing transactions, and in the preparation of financial statements.

Financial accounting information must be assembled and reported objectively.

a. General ledger
b. Current asset
c. Generally accepted accounting principles
d. Long-term liabilities

9. _____, in law and economics, is a form of risk management primarily used to hedge against the risk of a contingent loss. _____ is defined as the equitable transfer of the risk of a loss, from one entity to another, in exchange for a premium, and can be thought of as a guaranteed small loss to prevent a large, possibly devastating loss. An insurer is a company selling the _____; an insured is the person or entity buying the _____.

a. ABC Television Network
b. AIG
c. AMEX
d. Insurance

10. In business and accounting, _____ are everything of value that is owned by a person or company. It is a claim on the property your income of a borrower. The balance sheet of a firm records the monetary value of the _____ owned by the firm.

a. Accounts receivable
b. Assets
c. Earnings before interest, taxes, depreciation and amortization
d. Accrual basis accounting

11. In economics, _____ or _____ goods or real _____ refers to factors of production used to create goods or services that are not themselves significantly consumed (though they may depreciate) in the production process. _____ goods may be acquired with money or financial _____. In finance and accounting, _____ generally refers to financial wealth, especially that used to start or maintain a business.

a. Vyborg Appeal
b. Capital
c. Screening
d. Disclosure

12. In accounting, a _____ is an asset on the balance sheet which is expected to be sold or otherwise used up in the near future, usually within one year, or one business cycle - whichever is longer. Typical _____s include cash, cash equivalents, accounts receivable, inventory, the portion of prepaid accounts which will be used within a year, and short-term investments.

On the balance sheet, assets will typically be classified into _____s and long-term assets.

a. General ledger
b. Deferred
c. Pro forma
d. Current asset

13. In financial accounting, a _____ is defined as an obligation of an entity arising from past transactions or events, the settlement of which may result in the transfer or use of assets, provision of services or other yielding of economic benefits in the future.

a. Liability
b. Corporate governance
c. False Claims Act
d. Vested

Chapter 11. International Accounting and the Global Economy

14. The _____ of a stock is a measure of the price paid for a share relative to the annual net income or profit earned by the firm per share. It is a financial ratio used for valuation: a higher _____ means that investors are paying more for each unit of net income, so the stock is more expensive compared to one with lower _____. The _____ has units of years, which can be interpreted as 'number of years of earnings to pay back purchase price', ignoring the time value of money.

   a. Sharpe ratio
   b. Capital employed
   c. Rate of return
   d. P/E ratio

15. _____ in economics and business is the result of an exchange and from that trade we assign a numerical monetary value to a good, service or asset. If Alice trades Bob 4 apples for an orange, the _____ of an orange is 4 apples. Inversely, the _____ of an apple is 1/4 oranges.

   a. Transactional Net Margin Method
   b. Discounts and allowances
   c. Price discrimination
   d. Price

16. _____ is a specific term used in companies' financial reporting from the company-whole point of view. Because that use excludes the effects of changing ownership interest, an economic measure of _____ is necessary for financial analysis from the shareholders' point of view

   _____ is defined by the Financial Accounting Standards Board, or FASB, as 'the change in equity [net assets] of a business enterprise during a period from transactions and other events and circumstances from nonowner sources. It includes all changes in equity during a period except those resulting from investments by owners and distributions to owners.'

   _____ is the sum of net income and other items that must bypass the income statement because they have not been realized, including items like an unrealized holding gain or loss from available for sale securities and foreign currency translation gains or losses.

   a. BNSF Railway
   b. Comprehensive income
   c. 3M Company
   d. BMC Software, Inc.

17. An _____ is a practitioner of accountancy, which is the measurement, disclosure or provision of assurance about financial information that helps managers, investors, tax authorities and other decision makers make resource allocation decisions.

   The word '_____' is derived from the French 'Compter' which took its origin from the Latin 'Computare'. The word was formerly written in English as 'Accomptant', but in process of time the word, which was always pronounced by dropping the 'p', became gradually changed both in pronunciation and in orthography to its present form.

   a. AMEX
   b. ABC Television Network
   c. Accountant
   d. AIG

Chapter 11. International Accounting and the Global Economy

18. _____ is the title used by members of certain professional accountancy associations in the British Commonwealth countries and Ireland. The term chartered comes from the Royal Charter granted to the world's first professional body of accountants upon their establishment in 1854. The Edinburgh Society of Accountants (formed 1854), the Glasgow Institute of Accountants and Actuaries (1854) and the Aberdeen Society of Accountants (1867) were each granted a royal charter almost from their inception.

   a. Certified public accountant
   b. Chartered Accountant
   c. Chartered Certified Accountant
   d. Certified General Accountant

19. _____ is an acronym for First In, First Out, an abstraction in ways of organizing and manipulation of data relative to time and prioritization. This expression describes the principle of a queue processing technique or servicing conflicting demands by ordering process by first-come, first-served (FCFS) behaviour: what comes in first is handled first, what comes in next waits until the first is finished, etc.

   Thus it is analogous to the behaviour of persons queueing (or 'standing in line', in common American parlance), where the persons leave the queue in the order they arrive, or waiting one's turn at a traffic control signal.

   a. FIFO
   b. Risk management
   c. Kanban
   d. Trademark

20. _____ methods are means of managing inventory and financial matters involving the money a company ties up within inventory of produced goods, raw materials, parts, components, or feed stocks. FIFO stands for first-in, first-out, meaning that the oldest inventory items are recorded as sold first. LIFO stands for last-in, first-out, meaning that the most recently purchased items are recorded as sold first.

   a. Reorder point
   b. 3M Company
   c. Finished good
   d. FIFO and LIFO accounting

21. _____ is a common concept in economics, and gives rise to derived concepts such as consumer debt. Generally _____ is defined by opposition to production. But the precise definition can vary because different schools of economists define production quite differently.

   a. Consumption
   b. Yield
   c. Mitigating Control
   d. Starving the beast

22. The phrase _____, according to the Organization for Economic Co-operation and Development, refers to 'creative work undertaken on a systematic basis in order to increase the stock of knowledge, including knowledge of man, culture and society, and the use of this stock of knowledge to devise new applications [sic]'

   New product design and development is more than often a crucial factor in the survival of a company. In an industry that is fast changing, firms must continually revise their design and range of products. This is necessary due to continuous technology change and development as well as other competitors and the changing preference of customers.

   a. 3M Company
   b. BMC Software, Inc.
   c. BNSF Railway
   d. Research and development

23. _____ is a term used in accounting, economics and finance to spread the cost of an asset over the span of several years.

Chapter 11. International Accounting and the Global Economy

In simple words we can say that _____ is the reduction in the value of an asset due to usage, passage of time, wear and tear, technological outdating or obsolescence, depletion, inadequacy, rot, rust, decay or other such factors.

In accounting, _____ is a term used to describe any method of attributing the historical or purchase cost of an asset across its useful life, roughly corresponding to normal wear and tear.

a. Depreciation
b. Net profit
c. Current asset
d. General ledger

24. _____, also known as property, plant, and equipment (PP&E), is a term used in accountancy for assets and property which cannot easily be converted into cash. This can be compared with current assets such as cash or bank accounts, which are described as liquid assets. In most cases, only tangible assets are referred to as fixed.

a. Bankruptcy prediction
b. Fixed asset
c. Minority interest
d. Subledger

25. The _____ of 1977 (15 U.S.C. §§ 78dd-1, et seq.) is a United States federal law known primarily for two of its main provisions, one that addresses accounting transparency requirements under the Securities Exchange Act of 1934 and another concerning bribery of foreign officials.

a. Pre-emption right
b. Lease
c. Competition law
d. Foreign Corrupt Practices Act

26. A _____ is an annual report required by the U.S. Securities and Exchange Commission (SEC), that gives a comprehensive summary of a public company's performance. Although similarly named, the annual report on _____ is distinct from the often glossy 'annual report to shareholders', which a company must send to its shareholders when it holds an annual meeting to elect directors (though some companies combine the annual report and the 10-K into one document.) The 10-K includes information such as company history, organizational structure, executive compensation, equity, subsidiaries, and audited financial statements, among other information.

a. 3M Company
b. Form 10-Q
c. Form 8-K
d. Form 10-K

27. _____ is an SEC filing submitted to the US Securities and Exchange Commission used by certain foreign private issuers to provide information.

20-F, 20-F/A Annual and transition report of foreign private issuers pursuant to sections 13 or 15(d)

20FR12B, 20FR12B/A Form for initial registration of a class of securities of foreign private issuers pursuant to section 12(b)

20FR12G, 20FR12G/A Form for initial registration of a class of securities of foreign private issuers pursuant to section 12(g)

The postfix /A stands for 'Amendment'

Chapter 11. International Accounting and the Global Economy

The report must be filed within six months after the end of the fiscal year.

a. Form 10-Q
b. 3M Company
c. Form 8-K
d. Form 20-F

28. The U.S. _____ is an independent agency of the United States government which holds primary responsibility for enforcing the federal securities laws and regulating the securities industry, the nation's stock and options exchanges, and other electronic securities markets. The SEC was created by section 4 of the Securities Exchange Act of 1934 (now codified as 15 U.S.C. ÂÂ§ 78d and commonly referred to as the 1934 Act.)

a. Securities and Exchange Commission
b. BNSF Railway
c. 3M Company
d. BMC Software, Inc.

29. A _____ is a fungible, negotiable instrument representing financial value. they are broadly categorized into debt securities (such as banknotes, bonds and debentures), and equity securities; e.g., common stocks. The company or other entity issuing the _____ is called the issuer.

a. BMC Software, Inc.
b. Tracking stock
c. 3M Company
d. Security

30. An American Depository Receipt (or _____) represents the ownership in the shares of a foreign company trading on US financial markets. The stock of many non-US companies trades on US exchanges through the use of _____s. American Depository Receiptss enable US investors to buy shares in foreign companies without undertaking cross-border transactions.

a. ABC Television Network
b. American Depository Receipts
c. AMEX
d. AIG

31. NYSE Amex Equities, formerly known as the _____ is an _____ situated in New York. AMEX was a mutual organization, owned by its members. Until 1953 it was known as the New York Curb Exchange.

a. AIG
b. AMEX
c. ABC Television Network
d. American Stock Exchange

32. _____ was an American financier, banker and art collector who dominated corporate finance and industrial consolidation during his time. In 1892 Morgan arranged the merger of Edison General Electric and Thompson-Houston Electric Company to form General Electric. After financing the creation of the Federal Steel Company he merged the Carnegie Steel Company and several other steel and iron businesses to form the United States Steel Corporation in 1901.

a. Abby Joseph Cohen
b. Arthur Betz Laffer
c. Alan Greenspan
d. John Pierpont Morgan

33. The _____ (acronym of National Association of Securities Dealers Automated Quotations) is an American stock exchange. It is the largest electronic screen-based equity securities trading market in the United States. With approximately 3,800 companies, it has more trading volume per hour than any other stock exchange in the world.

a. Variance
b. Sustainability measurement
c. Sale of goods
d. NASDAQ

34. A _____ is any one of a variety of different systems, institutions, procedures, social relations and infrastructures whereby persons trade, and goods and services are exchanged, forming part of the economy. It is an arrangement that allows buyers and sellers to exchange things. _____s vary in size, range, geographic scale, location, types and variety of human communities, as well as the types of goods and services traded.
   a. Market Failure
   b. Perfect competition
   c. Market
   d. Recession

Chapter 12. Accounting for Foreign Currency Transactions and Hedging Foreign Exchange Risk

1. In monetary economics _____ can refer either to a particular _____, for example British Pounds or United States Dollars, or, to the coins and banknotes of a particular _____, which actually form only a small part of the monetary base of a nation's money supply. The other part of a nation's money supply consists of money deposited in banks (sometimes called deposit money), ownership of which can be transferred by means of checks (cheques in the United Kingdom and Australia) or other forms of money transfer such as credit and debit cards. Deposit money and _____ are 'money' in the sense that both are acceptable as a means of exchange, but money need not necessarily be '_____'.
   a. Currency
   b. BMC Software, Inc.
   c. BNSF Railway
   d. 3M Company

2. The _____ (CBOE), located at 400 South LaSalle Street in Chicago, is the largest U.S. options exchange with annual trading volume that hovered around one billion contracts at the end of 2007. _____ offers options on over 2,200 companies, 22 stock indexes, and 140 exchange-traded funds (ETFs.)

   The exchange, regulated by the Securities and Exchange Commission, was established in 1973.

   a. CBOE
   b. 3M Company
   c. Chicago Board Options Exchange
   d. BMC Software, Inc.

3. The _____ , located at 400 South LaSalle Street in Chicago, is the largest U.S. options exchange with annual trading volume that hovered around one billion contracts at the end of 2007. _____ offers options on over 2,200 companies, 22 stock indexes, and 140 exchange-traded funds (ETFs.)

   The exchange, regulated by the Securities and Exchange Commission, was established in 1973.

   a. Chicago Board Options Exchange
   b. 3M Company
   c. BMC Software, Inc.
   d. Pacific Exchange

4. The _____ , established in 1848, is the world's oldest futures and options exchange. More than 50 different options and futures contracts are traded by over 3,600 _____ members through open outcry and eTrading. Volumes at the exchange in 2003 were a record breaking 454 million contracts.
   a. BNSF Railway
   b. BMC Software, Inc.
   c. 3M Company
   d. Chicago Board of Trade

5. The _____ (often called 'the Chicago Merc,' or 'the Merc') is an American financial and commodity derivative exchange based in Chicago. The _____ was founded in 1898 as the Chicago Butter and Egg Board. Originally, the exchange was a non-profit organization.
   a. Public Company Accounting Oversight Board
   b. Financial Crimes Enforcement Network
   c. 3M Company
   d. Chicago Mercantile Exchange

6. In finance, an _____ is a contract between a buyer and a seller that gives the buyer the right--but not the obligation-- to buy or to sell a particular asset (the underlying asset) at a later time at an agreed price. In return for granting the _____, the seller collects a payment (the premium) from the buyer. A call _____ gives the buyer the right to buy the underlying asset; a put _____ gives the buyer of the _____ the right to sell the underlying asset.
   a. AIG
   b. ABC Television Network
   c. AMEX
   d. Option

Chapter 12. Accounting for Foreign Currency Transactions and Hedging Foreign Exchange Risk

7. _____ is a concept that denotes the precise probability of specific eventualities. Technically, the notion of _____ is independent from the notion of value and, as such, eventualities may have both beneficial and adverse consequences. However, in general usage the convention is to focus only on potential negative impact to some characteristic of value that may arise from a future event.
   - a. Discount factor
   - b. Discounting
   - c. Risk adjusted return on capital
   - d. Risk

8. _____ is activity directed towards the assessing, mitigating (to an acceptable level) and monitoring of risks. In some cases the acceptable risk may be near zero. Risks can come from accidents, natural causes and disasters as well as deliberate attacks from an adversary.
   - a. FIFO
   - b. Kanban
   - c. Trademark
   - d. Risk management

9. _____ is concerned with the provisions and use of accounting information to managers within organizations, to provide them with the basis to make informed business decisions that will allow them to be better equipped in their management and control functions.

   In contrast to financial accountancy information, _____ information is:

   - usually confidential and used by management, instead of publicly reported;
   - forward-looking, instead of historical;
   - pragmatically computed using extensive management information systems and internal controls, instead of complying with accounting standards.

   This is because of the different emphasis: _____ information is used within an organization, typically for decision-making.

   - a. Grenzplankostenrechnung
   - b. Governmental accounting
   - c. Management Accounting
   - d. Nonassurance services

10. In finance, the _____ between two currencies specifies how much one currency is worth in terms of the other. It is the value of a foreign nation's currency in terms of the home nation's currency. For example an _____ of 102 Japanese yen to the United States dollar means that JPY 102 is worth the same as USD 1.
    - a. AMEX
    - b. AIG
    - c. ABC Television Network
    - d. Exchange rate

11. _____ is an equity (stock) exchange located at 11 Wall Street in lower Manhattan, New York, USA.) It is the largest stock exchange in the world by dollar value of its listed companies' securities. As of October 2008, the combined capitalization of all domestic _____ listed companies was US$10.1 trillion.
    - a. BNSF Railway
    - b. BMC Software, Inc.
    - c. 3M Company
    - d. New York Stock Exchange

Chapter 12. Accounting for Foreign Currency Transactions and Hedging Foreign Exchange Risk

12. A _____, (formerly a securities exchange) is a corporation or mutual organization which provides 'trading' facilities for stock brokers and traders, to trade stocks and other securities. _____s also provide facilities for the issue and redemption of securities as well as other financial instruments and capital events including the payment of income and dividends. The securities traded on a _____ include: shares issued by companies, unit trusts, derivatives, pooled investment products and bonds.

   a. 3M Company
   b. BMC Software, Inc.
   c. BNSF Railway
   d. Stock Exchange

13. _____ is a form of risk that arises from the change in price of one currency against another. Whenever investors or companies have assets or business operations across national borders, they face _____ if their positions are not hedged.

   - Transaction risk is the risk that exchange rates will change unfavourably over time. It can be hedged against using forward currency contracts;
   - Translation risk is an accounting risk, proportional to the amount of assets held in foreign currencies. Changes in the exchange rate over time will render a report inaccurate, and so assets are usually balanced by borrowings in that currency.

The exchange risk associated with a foreign denominated instrument is a key element in foreign investment. This risk flows from differential monetary policy and growth in real productivity, which results in differential inflation rates.

   a. 3M Company
   b. Credit risk
   c. Currency risk
   d. Market risk

14. _____ is a file or account that contains money that a person or company owes to suppliers, but has not paid yet (a form of debt.) When you receive an invoice you add it to the file, and then you remove it when you pay. Thus, the A/P is a form of credit that suppliers offer to their purchasers by allowing them to pay for a product or service after it has already been received.

   a. Accounts receivable
   b. Accrual
   c. Earnings before interest, taxes, depreciation and amortization
   d. Accounts payable

15. _____ is one of a series of accounting transactions dealing with the billing of customers who owe money to a person, company or organization for goods and services that have been provided to the customer. In most business entities this is typically done by generating an invoice and mailing or electronically delivering it to the customer, who in turn must pay it within an established timeframe called credit or payment terms.

An example of a common payment term is Net 30, meaning payment is due in the amount of the invoice 30 days from the date of invoice.

   a. Adjusting entries
   b. Accrual
   c. Accrued revenue
   d. Accounts receivable

Chapter 12. Accounting for Foreign Currency Transactions and Hedging Foreign Exchange Risk

16. In finance, _____ is the process of estimating the potential market value of a financial asset or liability. They can be done on assets (for example, investments in marketable securities such as stocks, options, business enterprises, or intangible assets such as patents and trademarks) or on liabilities (e.g., Bonds issued by a company.) A _____ is required in many contexts including investment analysis, capital budgeting, merger and acquisition transactions, financial reporting, taxable events to determine the proper tax liability, and in litigation.
    a. Disclosure
    b. Valuation
    c. Daybook
    d. Vyborg Appeal

17. _____ is a fee paid on borrowed assets. It is the price paid for the use of borrowed money, or, money earned by deposited funds. Assets that are sometimes lent with _____ include money, shares, consumer goods through hire purchase, major assets such as aircraft, and even entire factories in finance lease arrangements. The _____ is calculated upon the value of the assets in the same manner as upon money.
    a. Insolvency
    b. Interest
    c. AIG
    d. ABC Television Network

18. An _____ is the price a borrower pays for the use of money they do not own, for instance a small company might borrow from a bank to kick start their business, and the return a lender receives for deferring the use of funds, by lending it to the borrower. _____s are normally expressed as a percentage rate over the period of one year.

    _____s targets are also a vital tool of monetary policy and are used to control variables like investment, inflation, and unemployment.

    a. AIG
    b. Interest rate
    c. AMEX
    d. ABC Television Network

19. In financial accounting, a _____ is defined as an obligation of an entity arising from past transactions or events, the settlement of which may result in the transfer or use of assets, provision of services or other yielding of economic benefits in the future.
    a. Vested
    b. False Claims Act
    c. Corporate governance
    d. Liability

20. In business and accounting, _____ are everything of value that is owned by a person or company. It is a claim on the property your income of a borrower. The balance sheet of a firm records the monetary value of the _____ owned by the firm.
    a. Earnings before interest, taxes, depreciation and amortization
    b. Accrual basis accounting
    c. Accounts receivable
    d. Assets

21. _____, also called fair price (in a commonplace conflation of the two distinct concepts), is a concept used in finance and economics, defined as a rational and unbiased estimate of the potential market price of a good, service, or asset, taking into account such objective factors as:

    - acquisition/production/distribution costs, replacement costs, or costs of close substitutes
    - actual utility at a given level of development of social productive capability
    - supply vs. demand

Chapter 12. Accounting for Foreign Currency Transactions and Hedging Foreign Exchange Risk

and subjective factors such as

- risk characteristics
- cost of capital
- individually perceived utility

In accounting, _____ is used as an estimate of the market value of an asset (or liability) for which a market price cannot be determined (usually because there is no established market for the asset.) Under GAAP (FAS 157), _____ is the amount at which the asset could be bought or sold in a current transaction between willing parties, or transferred to an equivalent party, other than in a liquidation sale. This is used for assets whose carrying value is based on mark-to-market valuations; for assets carried at historical cost, the _____ of the asset is not used. One example of where _____ is an issue is a College kitchen with a cost of $2 million which was built 5 years ago.

a. Fair value
c. 3M Company
b. BNSF Railway
d. BMC Software, Inc.

22. _____ is a financial mechanism in which a debtor obtains the right to delay payments to a creditor, for a defined period of time, in exchange for a charge or fee. Essentially, the party that owes money in the present purchases the right to delay the payment until some future date. The discount, or charge, is simply the difference between the original amount owed in the present and the amount that has to be paid in the future to settle the debt.

a. Discounting
c. Risk aversion
b. Risk adjusted return on capital
d. Discount factor

23. _____ is the balance of the amounts of cash being received and paid by a business during a defined period of time, sometimes tied to a specific project. Measurement of _____ can be used

- to evaluate the state or performance of a business or project.
- to determine problems with liquidity. Being profitable does not necessarily mean being liquid. A company can fail because of a shortage of cash, even while profitable.
- to project rate of returns. The time of _____s into and out of projects are used as inputs to financial models such as internal rate of return, and net present value.
- to examine income or growth of a business when it is believed that accrual accounting concepts do not represent economic realities. Alternately, _____ can be used to 'validate' the net income generated by accrual accounting.

_____ as a generic term may be used differently depending on context, and certain _____ definitions may be adapted by analysts and users for their own uses. Common terms include operating _____ and free _____.

a. Commercial paper
c. Controlling interest
b. Flow-through entity
d. Cash flow

Chapter 12. Accounting for Foreign Currency Transactions and Hedging Foreign Exchange Risk

24. A _____ is a hedge of the exposure to the variability of cash flow that

    1. is attributable to a particular risk associated with a recognized asset or liability. Such as all or some future interest payments on variable rate debt or a highly probable forecast transaction and
    2. could affect profit or loss

    a. Currency risk
    c. 3M Company
    b. Credit risk
    d. Cash flow Hedge

25. _____ means the giving out of information, either voluntarily or to be in compliance with legal regulations or workplace rules.

    - In Computer security, full _____ means disclosing full information about vulnerabilities.
    - In computing, _____ widget
    - Journalism, full _____ refers to disclosing the interests of the writer which may bear on the subject being written about, for example, if the writer has worked with an interview subject in the past.

    - In law:
        - The law of England and Wales, _____ refers to a process that may form part of legal proceedings, whereby parties inform to other parties the existence of any relevant documents that are, or have been, in their control. This compares with the process known as discovery in the course of legal proceedings in the United States.
        - In U.S. civil procedure (litigation rules for civil cases), _____ is a stage prior to trial. In civil cases, each party must disclose to the opposing party the following: names of witnesses which it may use to support its side, copies of documents (or mere description of these documents) in its control which it may use to support its side, computation of damages claimed, and certain insurance information. _____ is related to, but technically prior to, the discovery stage.
        - In Company law (known as 'corporate law' in the United States), _____ refers to giving out information about public or limited companies or their officers, which might be kept secret if the company was a private company or a partnership.

    - In real property transactions, _____ refers to providing to a buyer information known to the seller or broker/agent concerning the condition or other aspects of real property that would affect the property's value or desirability. These rules regarding what information must be disclosed, and whether the information must be disclosed even if a buyer does not ask, vary from one jurisdiction to the next.

    a. Tax harmonisation
    c. Trailing
    b. Disclosure
    d. Controlled Foreign Corporations

26. Most patent law systems require that a patent application disclose a claimed invention in sufficient detail for the notional person skilled in the art to carry out that claimed invention. This requirement is often known as sufficiency of disclosure or enablement, depending on the jurisdiction.

Chapter 12. Accounting for Foreign Currency Transactions and Hedging Foreign Exchange Risk

The _____ lies at the heart and origin of patent law. A state or government grants an inventor, or the inventor's assignee, a monopoly for a given period of time in exchange for the inventor disclosing to the public how to make or practice his or her invention. If a patent fails to contain such information, then the bargain is violated, and the patent is unenforceable.

a. False Claims Act
c. Tax patent

b. Pre-emption right
d. Disclosure requirement

27. A _____ is a financial contract between two parties, the buyer and the seller of this type of option. It is the option to buy shares of stock at a specified time in the future.Often it is simply labeled a 'call'. The buyer of the option has the right, but not the obligation to buy an agreed quantity of a particular commodity or financial instrument (the underlying instrument) from the seller of the option at a certain time (the expiration date) for a certain price (the strike price.)

a. Call option
c. Strike price

b. 3M Company
d. BMC Software, Inc.

28. A _____ is a financial contract between two parties, the seller (writer) and the buyer of the option. The buyer acquires a long position offering the right, but not obligation, to sell the underlying instrument at an agreed-upon price (the strike price.) If the buyer exercises the right granted by the option, the writer has the obligation to purchase the underlying at the strike price.

a. Put option
c. BMC Software, Inc.

b. Strike price
d. 3M Company

Chapter 13. Translation of Financial Statements of Foreign Affiliates

1. In monetary economics _____ can refer either to a particular _____, for example British Pounds or United States Dollars, or, to the coins and banknotes of a particular _____, which actually form only a small part of the monetary base of a nation's money supply. The other part of a nation's money supply consists of money deposited in banks (sometimes called deposit money), ownership of which can be transferred by means of checks (cheques in the United Kingdom and Australia) or other forms of money transfer such as credit and debit cards. Deposit money and _____ are 'money' in the sense that both are acceptable as a means of exchange, but money need not necessarily be '_____'.
   a. BMC Software, Inc.
   b. 3M Company
   c. BNSF Railway
   d. Currency

2. In finance, the _____ between two currencies specifies how much one currency is worth in terms of the other. It is the value of a foreign nation's currency in terms of the home nation's currency. For example an _____ of 102 Japanese yen to the United States dollar means that JPY 102 is worth the same as USD 1.
   a. AMEX
   b. Exchange rate
   c. ABC Television Network
   d. AIG

3. The _____ is a private, not-for-profit organization whose primary purpose is to develop generally accepted accounting principles (GAAP) within the United States in the public's interest. The Securities and Exchange Commission (SEC) designated the _____ as the organization responsible for setting accounting standards for public companies in the U.S. It was created in 1973, replacing the Accounting Principles Board and the Committee on Accounting Procedure of the American Institute of Certified Public Accountants. The _____'s mission is 'to establish and improve standards of financial accounting and reporting for the guidance and education of the public, including issuers, auditors, and users of financial information.'

   The _____ is not a governmental body.

   a. Governmental Accounting Standards Board
   b. Fannie Mae
   c. Financial Accounting Standards Board
   d. Public company

4. In economics, a _____, in its common usage, is a currency not backed by a national government (and not necessarily legal tender), and intended to trade only in a small area. These currencies are also referred to as community currency, or complementary currency. They encompass a wide range of forms, both physically and financially, and often are associated with a particular economic discourse.
   a. BNSF Railway
   b. BMC Software, Inc.
   c. 3M Company
   d. Local currency

5. _____ are formal records of a business' financial activities.

   In British English, including United Kingdom company law, _____ are often referred to as accounts, although the term _____ is also used, particularly by accountants.

   _____ provide an overview of a business' financial condition in both short and long term.

   a. Financial statements
   b. 3M Company
   c. Notes to the financial statements
   d. Statement of retained earnings

Chapter 13. Translation of Financial Statements of Foreign Affiliates

6. _____ is a specific term used in companies' financial reporting from the company-whole point of view. Because that use excludes the effects of changing ownership interest, an economic measure of _____ is necessary for financial analysis from the shareholders' point of view

_____ is defined by the Financial Accounting Standards Board, or FASB, as 'the change in equity [net assets] of a business enterprise during a period from transactions and other events and circumstances from nonowner sources. It includes all changes in equity during a period except those resulting from investments by owners and distributions to owners.'

_____ is the sum of net income and other items that must bypass the income statement because they have not been realized, including items like an unrealized holding gain or loss from available for sale securities and foreign currency translation gains or losses.

a. BMC Software, Inc.
b. BNSF Railway
c. 3M Company
d. Comprehensive income

7. _____ is the monetary unit of account of the principal economic environment in which an economic entity operates.

Statement of Financial Standards No. 52 (SFAS 52) is the primary source of GAAP for translation of foreign currency financial statements.

a. 3M Company
b. BMC Software, Inc.
c. Functional currency
d. BNSF Railway

Chapter 13. Translation of Financial Statements of Foreign Affiliates

8. _____ means the giving out of information, either voluntarily or to be in compliance with legal regulations or workplace rules.

- In Computer security, full _____ means disclosing full information about vulnerabilities.
- In computing, _____ widget
- Journalism, full _____ refers to disclosing the interests of the writer which may bear on the subject being written about, for example, if the writer has worked with an interview subject in the past.

- In law:
    - The law of England and Wales, _____ refers to a process that may form part of legal proceedings, whereby parties inform to other parties the existence of any relevant documents that are, or have been, in their control. This compares with the process known as discovery in the course of legal proceedings in the United States.
    - In U.S. civil procedure (litigation rules for civil cases), _____ is a stage prior to trial. In civil cases, each party must disclose to the opposing party the following: names of witnesses which it may use to support its side, copies of documents (or mere description of these documents) in its control which it may use to support its side, computation of damages claimed, and certain insurance information. _____ is related to, but technically prior to, the discovery stage.
    - In Company law (known as 'corporate law' in the United States), _____ refers to giving out information about public or limited companies or their officers, which might be kept secret if the company was a private company or a partnership.

- In real property transactions, _____ refers to providing to a buyer information known to the seller or broker/agent concerning the condition or other aspects of real property that would affect the property's value or desirability. These rules regarding what information must be disclosed, and whether the information must be disclosed even if a buyer does not ask, vary from one jurisdiction to the next.

a. Trailing
c. Tax harmonisation
b. Controlled Foreign Corporations
d. Disclosure

9. The _____ of 1977 (_____) (15 U.S.C. §§ 78dd-1, et seq.) is a United States federal law known primarily for two of its main provisions, one that addresses accounting transparency requirements under the Securities Exchange Act of 1934 and another concerning bribery of foreign officials.
   a. Federal Sentencing Guidelines
   c. Scottish Poor Laws
   b. Robinson-Patman Act
   d. FCPA

10. The _____ of 1977 (15 U.S.C. §§ 78dd-1, et seq.) is a United States federal law known primarily for two of its main provisions, one that addresses accounting transparency requirements under the Securities Exchange Act of 1934 and another concerning bribery of foreign officials.
    a. Competition law
    c. Foreign Corrupt Practices Act
    b. Pre-emption right
    d. Lease

11. A _____ is a fungible, negotiable instrument representing financial value. they are broadly categorized into debt securities (such as banknotes, bonds and debentures), and equity securities; e.g., common stocks. The company or other entity issuing the _____ is called the issuer.

a. 3M Company
b. BMC Software, Inc.
c. Security
d. Tracking stock

12. The U.S. _____ is an independent agency of the United States government which holds primary responsibility for enforcing the federal securities laws and regulating the securities industry, the nation's stock and options exchanges, and other electronic securities markets. The SEC was created by section 4 of the Securities Exchange Act of 1934 (now codified as 15 U.S.C. §§ 78d and commonly referred to as the 1934 Act.)

a. BMC Software, Inc.
b. BNSF Railway
c. Securities and Exchange Commission
d. 3M Company

13. An _____ is the buying of one company by another. An _____ may be friendly or hostile. In the former case, the companies cooperate in negotiations; in the latter case, the takeover target is unwilling to be bought or the target's board has no prior knowledge of the offer. _____ usually refers to a purchase of a smaller firm by a larger one. Sometimes, however, a smaller firm will acquire management control of a larger or longer established company and keep its name for the combined entity. This is known as a reverse takeover.

a. ABC Television Network
b. AIG
c. AMEX
d. Acquisition

14. _____ is generally understood in financial circles as the point at which revenue is recognized, typically through a transaction which involves the exchange of an asset, product, or service for cash or its equivalents.

This approach gives the accounting division a strictly objective basis for changing the books. For example, a homeowner may believe that his house has grown in value during a strong market, or fallen in value during a weak market, but until the house is actually sold for a specific price to a specific buyer, the change in value can only be estimated and is considered unrealized.

a. Valuation
b. Realization
c. Merck ' Co., Inc.
d. Total-factor productivity

15. In law, _____ refers to the process by which a company (or part of a company) is brought to an end, and the assets and property of the company redistributed. _____ can also be referred to as winding-up or dissolution, although dissolution technically refers to the last stage of _____. The process of _____ also arises when customs, an authority or agency in a country responsible for collecting and safeguarding customs duties, determines the final computation or ascertainment of the duties or drawback accruing on an entry.

a. Bankruptcy protection
b. BMC Software, Inc.
c. Liquidation
d. 3M Company

Chapter 14. Reporting for Segments and for Interim Financial Periods

1. The _____ is a private, not-for-profit organization whose primary purpose is to develop generally accepted accounting principles (GAAP) within the United States in the public's interest. The Securities and Exchange Commission (SEC) designated the _____ as the organization responsible for setting accounting standards for public companies in the U.S. It was created in 1973, replacing the Accounting Principles Board and the Committee on Accounting Procedure of the American Institute of Certified Public Accountants. The _____'s mission is 'to establish and improve standards of financial accounting and reporting for the guidance and education of the public, including issuers, auditors, and users of financial information.'

The _____ is not a governmental body.

a. Governmental Accounting Standards Board
b. Fannie Mae
c. Public company
d. Financial Accounting Standards Board

2. In economics, business, retail, and accounting, a _____ is the value of money that has been used up to produce something, and hence is not available for use anymore. In economics, a _____ is an alternative that is given up as a result of a decision. In business, the _____ may be one of acquisition, in which case the amount of money expended to acquire it is counted as _____.

a. Cost of quality
b. Prime cost
c. Cost allocation
d. Cost

3. In management accounting, _____ establishes budget and actual cost of operations, processes, departments or product and the analysis of variances, profitability or social use of funds. Managers use _____ to support decision-making to cut a company's costs and improve profitability. As a form of management accounting, _____ need not follow standards such as GAAP, because its primary use is for internal managers, rather than outside users, and what to compute is instead decided pragmatically.

a. Cost-volume-profit analysis
b. Cost Accounting
c. Prime cost
d. Marginal cost

4. In accounting, _____ has a very specific meaning. It is an outflow of cash or other valuable assets from a person or company to another person or company. This outflow of cash is generally one side of a trade for products or services that have equal or better current or future value to the buyer than to the seller.

a. Expense
b. AMEX
c. ABC Television Network
d. AIG

5. _____ are sometimes the same as net worth, or shareholders' equity - assets minus liabilities. The term _____ is commonly used with charities or not for profit entities. Although these entities don't make money, it is important to maintain reasonable reserves to help future growth.

a. Net assets
b. Sortino ratio
c. Debtor days
d. Net interest spread

6. _____ is one of the four Ps of the marketing mix. The other three aspects are product, promotion, and place. It is also a key variable in microeconomic price allocation theory.

a. Price
b. Cost-plus pricing
c. Target costing
d. Pricing

Chapter 14. Reporting for Segments and for Interim Financial Periods

7. _____ refers to the pricing of contributions (assets, tangible and intangible, services, and funds) transferred within an organization. For example, goods from the production division may be sold to the marketing division, or goods from a parent company may be sold to a foreign subsidiary. Since the prices are set within an organization (i.e. controlled), the typical market mechanisms that establish prices for such transactions between third parties may not apply.

   a. Transactional Net Margin Method
   b. Price
   c. Transfer pricing
   d. Pricing

8. In business and accounting, _____ are everything of value that is owned by a person or company. It is a claim on the property your income of a borrower. The balance sheet of a firm records the monetary value of the _____ owned by the firm.

   a. Accounts receivable
   b. Earnings before interest, taxes, depreciation and amortization
   c. Accrual basis accounting
   d. Assets

9. _____ is a process of attributing cost to particular cost centres. For example the wage of the driver of the purchasing department can be allocated to the purchasing department cost centre. It is not necessary to share the wage cost over several different cost centers.

   a. Variable cost
   b. Cost allocation
   c. Cost of quality
   d. Cost accounting

10. _____ is a measure of a company's earning power from ongoing operations, equal to earnings before the deduction of interest payments and income taxes.

    To accountants, economic profit, or EP, is a single-period metric to determine the value created by a company in one period - usually a year. It is the net profit after tax less the equity charge, a risk-weighted cost of capital.

    a. ABC Television Network
    b. Operating profit
    c. AMEX
    d. AIG

11. A _____, also client, buyer or purchaser is the buyer or user of the paid products of an individual or organization, mostly called the supplier or seller. This is typically through purchasing or renting goods or services.

    a. Customer
    b. 3M Company
    c. BMC Software, Inc.
    d. BNSF Railway

12. _____ was founded in June 1973 in London and replaced by the International Accounting Standards Board on April 1, 2001. It was responsible for developing the International Accounting Standards and promoting the use and application of these standards.

Chapter 14. Reporting for Segments and for Interim Financial Periods

The _____ was founded as a result of an agreement between accountancy bodies in the following countries:

- Australia (Institute of Chartered Accountants in Australia (ICAA) and the CPA Australia (formerly known as Australian Society of Certified Practising Accountants (ASCPA))

- Canada (Canadian Institute of Chartered Accountants (CICA))

- France (Ordre des Experts Comptable et des Comptables Agrees (Order of Accounting Experts and Qualified Accountants))

- Germany and the Wirtschaftsprüferkammer (WPK) (Chamber of Auditors))

- Japan Nihon Kouninkaikeishi Kyoukai)

- Mexico (Instituto Mexicano de Contadores Publicos (IMCP) (Mexican Institute of Public Accountants)) (removed from the board in 1987 due to non-payment of dues; resumed in 1995.)

- the Netherlands (Nederlands Instituut van Registeraccountants (NIVRA)

(Netherlands Institute of Registered Auditors))

- the United Kingdom and Ireland (counted as one) (Institute of Chartered Accountants in England and Wales (ICAEW), Institute of Chartered Accountants of Scotland (ICAS), Institute of Chartered Accountants in Ireland (ICAI), Association of Certified Accountants, Institute of Cost and Management Accountants, and the Institute of Municipal Treasurers and Accountants)

- the United States of America (American Institute of Certified Public Accountants (AICPA))

The Institute of Chartered Accountants of Nigeria became an associate member in 1976 and a member of the board from 1978 to 1987.

The National Council of Chartered Accountants (South Africa) became an associate member in 1974 and joined the board in 1978.

a. American Accounting Association
b. American Payroll Association
c. International Accounting Standards Board
d. International Accounting Standards Committee

13. The U.S. _____ is an independent agency of the United States government which holds primary responsibility for enforcing the federal securities laws and regulating the securities industry, the nation's stock and options exchanges, and other electronic securities markets. The SEC was created by section 4 of the Securities Exchange Act of 1934 (now codified as 15 U.S.C. ÂÂ§ 78d and commonly referred to as the 1934 Act.)

a. BMC Software, Inc.
b. 3M Company
c. BNSF Railway
d. Securities and Exchange Commission

Chapter 14. Reporting for Segments and for Interim Financial Periods

14. The _____ of 1977 (15 U.S.C. §§ 78dd-1, et seq.) is a United States federal law known primarily for two of its main provisions, one that addresses accounting transparency requirements under the Securities Exchange Act of 1934 and another concerning bribery of foreign officials.
    a. Foreign Corrupt Practices Act
    b. Lease
    c. Pre-emption right
    d. Competition law

15. A _____ is a fungible, negotiable instrument representing financial value. they are broadly categorized into debt securities (such as banknotes, bonds and debentures), and equity securities; e.g., common stocks. The company or other entity issuing the _____ is called the issuer.
    a. 3M Company
    b. Tracking stock
    c. BMC Software, Inc.
    d. Security

16. _____ were published by Accounting Principles Board (APB.) The board was created by American Institute of Certified Public Accountants (AICPA) in 1959 and was replaced by Financial Accounting Standards Board (FASB) in 1973. Its mission was to develop an overall conceptual framework of US generally accepted accounting principles (US GAAP.)
    a. AMEX
    b. ABC Television Network
    c. AIG
    d. Accounting Principles Board Opinions

17. _____, Quarterly Report Pursuant to Section 13 or 15(d) of the Securities Exchange Act of 1934, is an SEC filing that must be filed quarterly with the US Securities and Exchange Commission. It contains similar information to the annual form 10-K, however the information is generally less detailed, and the financial statements are generally unaudited. Information for the final quarter of a firm's fiscal year is included in the 10-K, so only three 10-Q filings are made each year.
    a. Form 20-F
    b. 3M Company
    c. Form 10-Q
    d. Form 8-K

Chapter 14. Reporting for Segments and for Interim Financial Periods

18. _____ means the giving out of information, either voluntarily or to be in compliance with legal regulations or workplace rules.

- In Computer security, full _____ means disclosing full information about vulnerabilities.
- In computing, _____ widget
- Journalism, full _____ refers to disclosing the interests of the writer which may bear on the subject being written about, for example, if the writer has worked with an interview subject in the past.

- In law:
    - The law of England and Wales, _____ refers to a process that may form part of legal proceedings, whereby parties inform to other parties the existence of any relevant documents that are, or have been, in their control. This compares with the process known as discovery in the course of legal proceedings in the United States.
    - In U.S. civil procedure (litigation rules for civil cases), _____ is a stage prior to trial. In civil cases, each party must disclose to the opposing party the following: names of witnesses which it may use to support its side, copies of documents (or mere description of these documents) in its control which it may use to support its side, computation of damages claimed, and certain insurance information. _____ is related to, but technically prior to, the discovery stage.
    - In Company law (known as 'corporate law' in the United States), _____ refers to giving out information about public or limited companies or their officers, which might be kept secret if the company was a private company or a partnership.

- In real property transactions, _____ refers to providing to a buyer information known to the seller or broker/agent concerning the condition or other aspects of real property that would affect the property's value or desirability. These rules regarding what information must be disclosed, and whether the information must be disclosed even if a buyer does not ask, vary from one jurisdiction to the next.

a. Tax harmonisation
c. Controlled Foreign Corporations
b. Trailing
d. Disclosure

19. The _____ is the national, professional association of CPAs in the United States, with more than 330,000 members, including CPAs in business and industry, public practice, government, and education; student affiliates; and international associates. It sets ethical standards for the profession and U.S. auditing standards for audits of private companies; federal, state and local governments; and non-profit organizations.

Approximately 40% of its members are engaged in the practice of public accounting, in areas such as auditing, accounting, taxation, general business consulting, business valuation, personal financial planning and business technology.

a. ABC Television Network
c. Other postemployment benefits
b. AIG
d. American Institute of Certified Public Accountants

20. An _____ is a practitioner of accountancy, which is the measurement, disclosure or provision of assurance about financial information that helps managers, investors, tax authorities and other decision makers make resource allocation decisions.

The word '_____' is derived from the French 'Compter' which took its origin from the Latin 'Computare'. The word was formerly written in English as 'Accomptant', but in process of time the word, which was always pronounced by dropping the 'p', became gradually changed both in pronunciation and in orthography to its present form.

   a. AIG
   b. AMEX
   c. ABC Television Network
   d. Accountant

21. The _____ is a professional organization headquartered in Montvale, New Jersey consisting of over 70,000 members worldwide. The IMA is dedicated to advancing the role of the management accountant and financial manager within the business organization, and provides relevant professional certification.

The IMA awards the Certified Management Accountant (CMA) designation in the United States.

   a. Institute of Management Accountants
   b. International Accounting Standards Committee
   c. Emerging technologies
   d. American Accounting Association

22. _____ is concerned with the provisions and use of accounting information to managers within organizations, to provide them with the basis to make informed business decisions that will allow them to be better equipped in their management and control functions.

In contrast to financial accountancy information, _____ information is:

- usually confidential and used by management, instead of publicly reported;
- forward-looking, instead of historical;
- pragmatically computed using extensive management information systems and internal controls, instead of complying with accounting standards.

This is because of the different emphasis: _____ information is used within an organization, typically for decision-making.

   a. Nonassurance services
   b. Grenzplankostenrechnung
   c. Governmental accounting
   d. Management accounting

23. A _____, (formerly a securities exchange) is a corporation or mutual organization which provides 'trading' facilities for stock brokers and traders, to trade stocks and other securities. _____s also provide facilities for the issue and redemption of securities as well as other financial instruments and capital events including the payment of income and dividends. The securities traded on a _____ include: shares issued by companies, unit trusts, derivatives, pooled investment products and bonds.

   a. BMC Software, Inc.
   b. 3M Company
   c. BNSF Railway
   d. Stock Exchange

Chapter 15. Partnerships: Formation, Operation, and Ownership Changes

1. A _____ is a type of business entity in which partners (owners) share with each other the profits or losses of the business undertaking in which all have invested. _____s are often favored over corporations for taxation purposes, as the _____ structure does not generally incur a tax on profits before it is distributed to the partners (i.e. there is no dividend tax levied.) However, depending on the _____ structure and the jurisdiction in which it operates, owners of a _____ may be exposed to greater personal liability than they would as shareholders of a corporation.
   a. National Information Infrastructure Protection Act
   b. Resource Conservation and Recovery Act
   c. Corporate governance
   d. Partnership

2. An _____ is a term used in behavioral economics to describe those types of behaviors that impose costs on a person in the long-run that are not taken into account when making decisions in the present. Classical Economics discourages government from creating legislation that targets internalities, because it is assumed that the consumer takes these personal costs into account when paying for the good that causes the _____. For example, cigarettes should be taxed because of the negative consumption externalities that they impose, such as second-hand smoke, not because the smoker harms him or herself by smoking.
   a. Operating budget
   b. Inventory turnover ratio
   c. Internality
   d. Authorised capital

3. The _____ is the United States federal government agency that collects taxes and enforces the internal revenue laws. It is an agency within the U.S. Dept of the treasury responsible for interpretation and application of Federal tax law. The official U.S. Treasury regulations provide (in part):

   The _____ is a bureau of the Department of the Treasury under the immediate direction of the Commissioner of Internal Revenue.

   a. Indirect tax
   b. Use tax
   c. Internal Revenue Service
   d. Income tax

4. In financial accounting, a _____ is defined as an obligation of an entity arising from past transactions or events, the settlement of which may result in the transfer or use of assets, provision of services or other yielding of economic benefits in the future.
   a. Corporate governance
   b. Vested
   c. False Claims Act
   d. Liability

5. _____ is a concept whereby a person's financial liability is limited to a fixed sum, most commonly the value of a person's investment in a company or partnership with _____. A shareholder in a limited company is not personally liable for any of the debts of the company, other than for the value of his investment in that company. The same is true for the members of a _____ partnership and the limited partners in a limited partnership.
   a. Burden of proof
   b. Joint venture
   c. Limited Liability
   d. Due diligence

6. A _____ in the law of the vast majority of United States jurisdictions is a legal form of business company that provides limited liability to its owners. Often incorrectly called a 'limited liability corporation' (instead of company), it is a hybrid business entity having certain characteristics of both a corporation and a partnership. The primary characteristic an _____ shares with a corporation is limited liability, and the primary characteristic it shares with a partnership is the availability of pass-through income taxation.

Chapter 15. Partnerships: Formation, Operation, and Ownership Changes

a. Bond market
b. Consumer protection laws
c. Data protection
d. Limited Liability Company

7. The _____ , which includes revisions that are sometimes called the Revised _____ , is a uniform act (similar to a model statute), proposed by the National Conference of Commissioners on Uniform State Laws ('NCCUSL') for the governance of business partnerships by U.S. States. Several versions of _____ have been promulgated by the NCCUSL, the earliest having been put forth in 1914, and the most recent in 1997.

The NCCUSL's first revision of _____ was promulgated in 1992 and amended in 1993 and 1994.

a. ABC Television Network
b. AMEX
c. AIG
d. Uniform Partnership Act

8. In the commercial and legal parlance of most countries, a _____ or simply a partnership, refers to an association of persons or an unincorporated company with the following major features:

- Created by agreement, proof of existence and estoppel.
- Formed by two or more persons
- The owners are all personally liable for any legal actions and debts the company may face

It is a partnership in which partners share equally in both responsibility and liability.

Partnerships have certain default characteristics relating to both the relationship between the individual partners and (b) the relationship between the partnership and the outside world. The former can generally be overridden by agreement between the partners, whereas the latter generally cannot be.

The assets of the business are owned on behalf of the other partners, and they are each personally liable, jointly and severally, for business debts, taxes or tortious liability.

a. Governmental Accounting Standards Board
b. General partnership
c. Multinational corporation
d. Dow Jones ' Company

9. A _____ is an entity formed between two or more parties to undertake economic activity together. The parties agree to create a new entity by both contributing equity, and they then share in the revenues, expenses, and control of the enterprise. The venture can be for one specific project only, or a continuing business relationship such as the Fuji Xerox _____ .

a. Chief Financial Officers Act of 1990
b. Pre-emption right
c. Fraud Enforcement and Recovery Act
d. Joint venture

10. A _____ is a form of partnership similar to a general partnership, except that in addition to one or more general partners (GPs), there are one or more limited partners (_____s.) It is a partnership in which only one partner is required to be a general partner.

The GPs are, in all major respects, in the same legal position as partners in a conventional firm, i.e. they have management control, share the right to use partnership property, share the profits of the firm in predefined proportions, and have joint and several liability for the debts of the partnership.

Chapter 15. Partnerships: Formation, Operation, and Ownership Changes

a. Minority interest
b. Dow Jones ' Company
c. Debenture
d. Limited Partnership

11. _____ is a voluntary contract between two or among more than two persons to place their capital, labor, and skills, and corporation in business with the understanding that there will be a sharing of the profits and losses between/among partners. Outside of North America, it is normally referred to simply as a partnership agreement.

There are also multiple sections which are often included as well in _____, based on the circumstance.

a. AIG
b. ABC Television Network
c. AMEX
d. Articles of partnership

12. In economics, _____ or _____ goods or real _____ refers to factors of production used to create goods or services that are not themselves significantly consumed (though they may depreciate) in the production process. _____ goods may be acquired with money or financial _____. In finance and accounting, _____ generally refers to financial wealth, especially that used to start or maintain a business.

a. Disclosure
b. Screening
c. Vyborg Appeal
d. Capital

13. _____ is a fee paid on borrowed assets. It is the price paid for the use of borrowed money, or, money earned by deposited funds. Assets that are sometimes lent with _____ include money, shares, consumer goods through hire purchase, major assets such as aircraft, and even entire factories in finance lease arrangements. The _____ is calculated upon the value of the assets in the same manner as upon money.

a. Insolvency
b. ABC Television Network
c. AIG
d. Interest

14. In finance, a _____ is a debt security, in which the authorized issuer owes the holders a debt and, depending on the terms of the _____, is obliged to pay interest (the coupon) and/or to repay the principal at a later date, termed maturity. It is a formal contract to repay borrowed money with interest at fixed intervals.

Thus a _____ is like a loan: the issuer is the borrower, the _____ holder is the lender, and the coupon is the interest.

a. Bond
b. Coupon rate
c. Revenue bonds
d. Zero-coupon bond

15. A _____ is a form of periodic payment from an employer to an employee, which may be specified in an employment contract. It is contrasted with piece wages, where each job, hour or other unit is paid separately, rather than on a periodic basis.

From the point of a view of running a business, _____ can also be viewed as the cost of acquiring human resources for running operations, and is then termed personnel expense or _____ expense.

a. 3M Company
b. Separation of duties
c. BMC Software, Inc.
d. Salary

16. _____ is the state or fact of exclusive rights and control over property, which may be an object, land/real estate or intellectual property. An _____ right is also referred to as title.

_____ is the key building block in the development of the capitalist socio-economic system.

a. Administrative proceeding
c. ABC Television Network
b. Encumbrance
d. Ownership

17. In finance, _____ is the process of estimating the potential market value of a financial asset or liability. They can be done on assets (for example, investments in marketable securities such as stocks, options, business enterprises, or intangible assets such as patents and trademarks) or on liabilities (e.g., Bonds issued by a company.) A _____ is required in many contexts including investment analysis, capital budgeting, merger and acquisition transactions, financial reporting, taxable events to determine the proper tax liability, and in litigation.

a. Vyborg Appeal
c. Disclosure
b. Daybook
d. Valuation

Chapter 16. Partnership Liquidation

1. In law, _____ refers to the process by which a company (or part of a company) is brought to an end, and the assets and property of the company redistributed. _____ can also be referred to as winding-up or dissolution, although dissolution technically refers to the last stage of _____. The process of _____ also arises when customs, an authority or agency in a country responsible for collecting and safeguarding customs duties, determines the final computation or ascertainment of the duties or drawback accruing on an entry.
   a. BMC Software, Inc.
   b. Bankruptcy protection
   c. 3M Company
   d. Liquidation

2. A _____ is a type of business entity in which partners (owners) share with each other the profits or losses of the business undertaking in which all have invested. _____s are often favored over corporations for taxation purposes, as the _____ structure does not generally incur a tax on profits before it is distributed to the partners (i.e. there is no dividend tax levied.) However, depending on the _____ structure and the jurisdiction in which it operates, owners of a _____ may be exposed to greater personal liability than they would as shareholders of a corporation.
   a. National Information Infrastructure Protection Act
   b. Resource Conservation and Recovery Act
   c. Corporate governance
   d. Partnership

3. The _____, which includes revisions that are sometimes called the Revised _____, is a uniform act (similar to a model statute), proposed by the National Conference of Commissioners on Uniform State Laws ('NCCUSL') for the governance of business partnerships by U.S. States. Several versions of _____ have been promulgated by the NCCUSL, the earliest having been put forth in 1914, and the most recent in 1997.

   The NCCUSL's first revision of _____ was promulgated in 1992 and amended in 1993 and 1994.

   a. ABC Television Network
   b. AIG
   c. AMEX
   d. Uniform Partnership Act

4. _____ are sometimes the same as net worth, or shareholders' equity - assets minus liabilities. The term _____ is commonly used with charities or not for profit entities. Although these entities don't make money, it is important to maintain reasonable reserves to help future growth.
   a. Net assets
   b. Net interest spread
   c. Debtor days
   d. Sortino ratio

5. In business and accounting, _____ are everything of value that is owned by a person or company. It is a claim on the property your income of a borrower. The balance sheet of a firm records the monetary value of the _____ owned by the firm.
   a. Accounts receivable
   b. Assets
   c. Earnings before interest, taxes, depreciation and amortization
   d. Accrual basis accounting

6. A _____ is the transfer of wealth from one party (such as a person or company) to another. A _____ is usually made in exchange for the provision of goods, services or both, or to fulfill a legal obligation.

   The simplest and oldest form of _____ is barter, the exchange of one good or service for another.

   a. 3M Company
   b. Payment
   c. BMC Software, Inc.
   d. Payee

Chapter 17. Introduction to Fund Accounting

1. _____ is an accounting system often used by nonprofit organizations and by the public sector. According to StartHereGoPlaces, _____ is a '[m]ethod of accounting and presentation whereby assets and liabilities are grouped according to the purpose for which they are to be used.'

   _____ serves any nonprofit organization or the public sector. These organizations have a need for special reporting to financial statements users that show how money is spent, rather than how much profit was earned.

   a. Replacement cost
   b. Liquidating dividend
   c. Refunding
   d. Fund accounting

2. _____ is the term used to refer to the standard framework of guidelines for financial accounting used in any given jurisdiction. _____ includes the standards, conventions, and rules accountants follow in recording and summarizing transactions, and in the preparation of financial statements.

   Financial accounting information must be assembled and reported objectively.

   a. Current asset
   b. Long-term liabilities
   c. General ledger
   d. Generally accepted accounting principles

3. The _____ (GAO) is the audit, evaluation, and investigative arm of the United States Congress. It is located in the Legislative branch of the United States government.

   The _____ was established as the _____ by the Budget and Accounting Act of 1921 (Pub.L.

   a. 3M Company
   b. General Accounting Office
   c. BMC Software, Inc.
   d. GAO

4. _____ is an umbrella term which refers to the various accounting systems used by various public sector entities. In the United States, for instance, there are two levels of government which follow different accounting standards set forth by independent, private sector boards. At the federal level, the Federal Accounting Standards Advisory Board (FASAB) sets forth the accounting standards to follow.

   a. Governmental accounting
   b. Management accounting
   c. Nonassurance services
   d. Product control

5. A _____ is a non-profit organization seeking to further a particular profession, the interests of individuals engaged in that profession, and the public interest.

   The roles of these _____s have been variously defined: 'A group of people in a learned occupation who are entrusted with maintaining control or oversight of the legitimate practice of the occupation;' also a body acting 'to safeguard the public interest;' organizations which 'represent the interest of the professional practitioners,' and so 'act to maintain their own privileged and powerful position as a controlling body.'

   Such bodies generally strive to achieve a balance between these two often conflicting mandates. Though professional bodies often act to protect the public by maintaining and enforcing standards of training and ethics in their profession, they often also act like a cartel or a labor union for the members of the profession, though this description is commonly rejected by the body concerned.

Chapter 17. Introduction to Fund Accounting 77

   a. MicroStrategy
   b. HFMA
   c. Professional association
   d. Freddie Mac

6. _____ are formal records of a business' financial activities.

In British English, including United Kingdom company law, _____ are often referred to as accounts, although the term _____ is also used, particularly by accountants.

_____ provide an overview of a business' financial condition in both short and long term.

   a. Financial statements
   b. Notes to the financial statements
   c. 3M Company
   d. Statement of retained earnings

7. _____ is financial assistance paid to people by governments. Some _____ is general, while specific and can only be invoked under certain circumstances, such as a scholarship. _____ payments can be made to individuals or to companies or entities--these latter payments are often considered corporate _____.

   a. Price-to-sales ratio
   b. Joseph Ronald Banister
   c. Swap
   d. Welfare

8. _____ is the process of increasing, or accounting for, an amount over a period of time. Particular instances of the term include:

- _____, the allocation of a lump sum amount to different time periods, particularly for loans and other forms of finance, including related interest or other finance charges.
    - _____ schedule, a table detailing each periodic payment on a loan (typically a mortgage), as generated by an _____ calculator.
    - Negative _____, an _____ schedule where the loan amount actually increases through not paying the full interest
- Amortized analysis, analyzing the execution cost of algorithms over a sequence of operations.
- _____ of capital expenditures of certain assets under accounting rules, particularly intangible assets, in a manner analogous to depreciation.
- _____

   a. EBIT
   b. Annuity
   c. Intangible
   d. Amortization

9. The word _____ indicates that a party, or proprietor, exercises private ownership, control or use over an item of property

   a. 3M Company
   b. Proprietary
   c. BMC Software, Inc.
   d. BNSF Railway

10. The _____ is the former authoritative body of the American Institute of Certified Public Accountants (AICPA.) It was created by the American Institute of Certified Public Accountants in 1959 and issued pronouncements on accounting principles until 1973, when it was replaced by the Financial Accounting Standards Board (FASB.)

Chapter 17. Introduction to Fund Accounting

The _____ was disbanded in the hopes that the smaller, fully-independent FASB could more effectively create accounting standards.

a. Accounting Principles Board
c. International Federation of Accountants
b. Institute of Management Accountants
d. American Payroll Association

11. _____ were published by Accounting Principles Board (APB.) The board was created by American Institute of Certified Public Accountants (AICPA) in 1959 and was replaced by Financial Accounting Standards Board (FASB) in 1973. Its mission was to develop an overall conceptual framework of US generally accepted accounting principles (US GAAP.)

a. Accounting Principles Board Opinions
c. ABC Television Network
b. AMEX
d. AIG

12. _____ is the act of taking possession of or assigning purpose to properties or ideas and is important in many topics, including:

- _____ in relation to the spread of knowledge
- _____ (art)
  - _____ (music) in reference to the re-use and proliferation of different types of music
- _____ (economics) origination of human ownership of previously unowned natural resources such as land
- _____ (law) as a component of government spending
- Cultural _____ is the borrowing, or theft, of an element of cultural expression of one group by another.
- The tort of _____ is one form of invasion of privacy.

a. Annuity
c. Appropriation
b. Intangible
d. Improvement

13. _____ of something is, in finance, the adding together of interest or different investments over a period of time such as atoms (1 - the act or process of accruing; 2 - the amount that accrues.) It holds specific meanings in accounting and payroll.

_____, in accounting, describes the accounting method known as _____ basis, whereby revenues and expenses are recognized when they are accrued, i.e. accumulated (earned or incurred), regardless when the actual cash is received or paid out.

a. Accrual
c. Assets
b. Earnings before interest, taxes, depreciation and amortization
d. Accounts receivable

14. _____ is a method of accounting whereby economic activities (rather than cash flow) of financial events are considered, because of two complementary principles, which (together) determine the point, at which expenses and revenues are recognized. According to revenue recognition principle, revenues are realized when earned, whether or not they are received in cash.

Chapter 17. Introduction to Fund Accounting

a. Earnings before interest, taxes, depreciation and amortization

b. Accrual

c. Accrued revenue

d. Accrual basis accounting

15. In finance, a _____ is a debt security, in which the authorized issuer owes the holders a debt and, depending on the terms of the _____, is obliged to pay interest (the coupon) and/or to repay the principal at a later date, termed maturity. It is a formal contract to repay borrowed money with interest at fixed intervals.

Thus a _____ is like a loan: the issuer is the borrower, the _____ holder is the lender, and the coupon is the interest.

a. Bond

b. Coupon rate

c. Revenue bonds

d. Zero-coupon bond

16. _____ is any physical or virtual entity that is owned by an individual or jointly by a group of individuals. An owner of _____ has the right to consume, sell, rent, mortgage, transfer and exchange his or her _____. Important widely-recognized types of _____ include real _____, personal _____ (other physical possessions), and intellectual _____ (rights over artistic creations, inventions, etc.), although the latter is not always as widely recognized or enforced.

a. Property

b. Disclosure requirement

c. Fiduciary

d. Primary authority

17. A _____ is the pinnacle activity involved in selling products or services in return for money or other compensation. It is an act of completion of a commercial activity.

A _____ is completed by the seller, the owner of the goods.

a. High yield stock

b. Maturity

c. Tertiary sector of economy

d. Sale

18. The American Oil Company founded in Baltimore in 1910 and incorporated in 1922 by Louis Blaustein and his son Jacob, but is now part of BP. The firm's innovations included two essential parts of the modern industry- the gasoline tanker truck and the drive-through filling station.

In 1923 the Blausteins sold a half interest in _____ to the Pan American Petroleum ' Transport company in exchange for a guaranteed supply of oil.

a. International Federation of Accountants

b. International Accounting Standards Committee

c. Amoco

d. Information Systems Audit and Control Association

19. _____ is a legal term of art for anything that affects or limits the title of a property, such as mortgages, leases, easements, liens, or restrictions. Also, those considered as potentially making the title defeasible are also _____s. For example, charging orders, building orders and structure alteration.

a. Ownership

b. ABC Television Network

c. Administrative proceeding

d. Encumbrance

Chapter 17. Introduction to Fund Accounting

20. In economics, _____ or _____ goods or real _____ refers to factors of production used to create goods or services that are not themselves significantly consumed (though they may depreciate) in the production process. _____ goods may be acquired with money or financial _____. In finance and accounting, _____ generally refers to financial wealth, especially that used to start or maintain a business.
    a. Disclosure
    b. Vyborg Appeal
    c. Screening
    d. Capital

21. A _____ is an expenditure creating future benefits. A _____ is incurred when a business spends money either to buy fixed assets or to add to the value of an existing fixed asset with a useful life that extends beyond the taxable year. Capex are used by a company to acquire or upgrade physical assets such as equipment, property, or industrial buildings.
    a. 3M Company
    b. Capital expenditure
    c. Cost of capital
    d. BMC Software, Inc.

22. The _____ is currently the source of generally accepted accounting principles (GAAP) used by State and Local governments in the [[United States of America]]. As with most of the entities involved in creating GAAP in the United States, it is a private, non-governmental organization.

    The _____ is subject to oversight by the Financial Accounting Foundation (FAF), which selects the members of the _____ and the Financial Accounting Standards Board, and funds both organizations.

    a. Fannie Mae
    b. National Conference of Commissioners on Uniform State Laws
    c. Multinational corporation
    d. Governmental Accounting Standards Board

23. _____ is a common concept in economics, and gives rise to derived concepts such as consumer debt. Generally _____ is defined by opposition to production. But the precise definition can vary because different schools of economists define production quite differently.
    a. Mitigating Control
    b. Consumption
    c. Yield
    d. Starving the beast

Chapter 18. Introduction to Accounting for State and Local Governmental Units

1. The _____ is currently the source of generally accepted accounting principles (GAAP) used by State and Local governments in the [[United States of America]]. As with most of the entities involved in creating GAAP in the United States, it is a private, non-governmental organization.

   The _____ is subject to oversight by the Financial Accounting Foundation (FAF), which selects the members of the _____ and the Financial Accounting Standards Board, and funds both organizations.

   a. National Conference of Commissioners on Uniform State Laws
   b. Multinational corporation
   c. Fannie Mae
   d. Governmental Accounting Standards Board

2. _____ is an umbrella term which refers to the various accounting systems used by various public sector entities. In the United States, for instance, there are two levels of government which follow different accounting standards set forth by independent, private sector boards. At the federal level, the Federal Accounting Standards Advisory Board (FASAB) sets forth the accounting standards to follow.

   a. Governmental accounting
   b. Product control
   c. Nonassurance services
   d. Management accounting

3. The _____ (or _____) is a professional association of state, provincial, and local government finance officers in the United States and Canada.

   The _____ sponsors award programs designed to encourage good financial reporting, for financial documents including the Comprehensive annual financial report, or CAFR, and the annual budget. They also sponsor the Frank L. Greathouse Government Scholarship each year for use by a college senior preparing for a career in state or local government finance.

   a. 3M Company
   b. BNSF Railway
   c. BMC Software, Inc.
   d. GFOA

4. An _____ is a practitioner of accountancy, which is the measurement, disclosure or provision of assurance about financial information that helps managers, investors, tax authorities and other decision makers make resource allocation decisions.

   The word '_____' is derived from the French 'Compter' which took its origin from the Latin 'Computare'. The word was formerly written in English as 'Accomptant', but in process of time the word, which was always pronounced by dropping the 'p', became gradually changed both in pronunciation and in orthography to its present form.

   a. Accountant
   b. AMEX
   c. ABC Television Network
   d. AIG

5. The _____ is the national, professional association of CPAs in the United States, with more than 330,000 members, including CPAs in business and industry, public practice, government, and education; student affiliates; and international associates. It sets ethical standards for the profession and U.S. auditing standards for audits of private companies; federal, state and local governments; and non-profit organizations.

Chapter 18. Introduction to Accounting for State and Local Governmental Units

Approximately 40% of its members are engaged in the practice of public accounting, in areas such as auditing, accounting, taxation, general business consulting, business valuation, personal financial planning and business technology.

a. AIG
b. ABC Television Network
c. Other postemployment benefits
d. American Institute of Certified Public Accountants

6. _____ is the statutory title of qualified accountants in the United States who have passed the Uniform _____ Examination and have met additional state education and experience requirements for certification as a _____. Individuals who have passed the Exam but have not either accomplished the required on-the-job experience or have previously met it but in the meantime have lapsed their continuing professional education are, in many states, permitted the designation '_____ Inactive' or an equivalent phrase. In most U.S. states, only _____s who are licensed are able to provide to the public attestation (including auditing) opinions on financial statements.

a. Chartered Accountant
b. Certified Public Accountant
c. Chartered Certified Accountant
d. Certified General Accountant

7. The _____ is located in Norwalk, Connecticut. It is an independent, organization in the private sector that is responsible for oversight of the Financial Accounting Standards Board (FASB), the Governmental Accounting Standards Board (GASB), and their respective advisory councils.

a. BNSF Railway
b. 3M Company
c. BMC Software, Inc.
d. Financial Accounting Foundation

8. A municipality is an administrative entity composed of a clearly defined territory and its population and commonly denotes a city, town or a small grouping of them. A municipality is typically governed by a mayor and a city council or _____ council.

The notion of municipality includes townships but is not restricted to them.

a. BMC Software, Inc.
b. 3M Company
c. BNSF Railway
d. Municipal

9. _____ is the process of increasing, or accounting for, an amount over a period of time. Particular instances of the term include:

- _____, the allocation of a lump sum amount to different time periods, particularly for loans and other forms of finance, including related interest or other finance charges.
  - _____ schedule, a table detailing each periodic payment on a loan (typically a mortgage), as generated by an _____ calculator.
  - Negative _____, an _____ schedule where the loan amount actually increases through not paying the full interest
- Amortized analysis, analyzing the execution cost of algorithms over a sequence of operations.
- _____ of capital expenditures of certain assets under accounting rules, particularly intangible assets, in a manner analogous to depreciation.
- _____

Chapter 18. Introduction to Accounting for State and Local Governmental Units

a. Annuity
c. EBIT
b. Intangible
d. Amortization

10. In economics, _____ or _____ goods or real _____ refers to factors of production used to create goods or services that are not themselves significantly consumed (though they may depreciate) in the production process. _____ goods may be acquired with money or financial _____. In finance and accounting, _____ generally refers to financial wealth, especially that used to start or maintain a business.
    a. Screening
    c. Vyborg Appeal
    b. Disclosure
    d. Capital

11. _____ is that which is owed; usually referencing assets owed, but the term can also cover moral obligations and other interactions not requiring money. In the case of assets, _____ is a means of using future purchasing power in the present before a summation has been earned. Some companies and corporations use _____ as a part of their overall corporate finance strategy.
    a. Debenture
    c. Loan
    b. Lender
    d. Debt

12. The _____ duty is a legal relationship of confidence or trust between two or more parties, most commonly a _____ or trustee and a principal or beneficiary. One party, for example a corporate trust company or the trust department of a bank, holds a _____ relation or acts in a _____ capacity to another, such as one whose funds are entrusted to it for investment. In a _____ relation one person justifiably reposes confidence, good faith, reliance and trust in another whose aid, advice or protection is sought in some matter.
    a. FCPA
    c. Robinson-Patman Act
    b. Fiduciary
    d. Staple right

13. An _____ is a term used in behavioral economics to describe those types of behaviors that impose costs on a person in the long-run that are not taken into account when making decisions in the present. Classical Economics discourages government from creating legislation that targets internalities, because it is assumed that the consumer takes these personal costs into account when paying for the good that causes the _____. For example, cigarettes should be taxed because of the negative consumption externalities that they impose, such as second-hand smoke, not because the smoker harms him or herself by smoking.
    a. Operating budget
    c. Authorised capital
    b. Inventory turnover ratio
    d. Internality

14. The word _____ indicates that a party, or proprietor, exercises private ownership, control or use over an item of property
    a. BNSF Railway
    c. Proprietary
    b. 3M Company
    d. BMC Software, Inc.

15. Employment is a contract between two parties, one being the employer and the other being the _____. An _____ may be defined as: 'A person in the service of another under any contract of hire, express or implied, oral or written, where the employer has the power or right to control and direct the _____ in the material details of how the work is to be performed.' Black's Law Dictionary page 471 (5th ed. 1979.)
    a. AIG
    c. Employee
    b. AMEX
    d. ABC Television Network

Chapter 18. Introduction to Accounting for State and Local Governmental Units

16. In business and accounting, _____ are everything of value that is owned by a person or company. It is a claim on the property your income of a borrower. The balance sheet of a firm records the monetary value of the _____ owned by the firm.

   a. Accounts receivable
   b. Earnings before interest, taxes, depreciation and amortization
   c. Accrual basis accounting
   d. Assets

17. _____, also known as property, plant, and equipment (PP&E), is a term used in accountancy for assets and property which cannot easily be converted into cash. This can be compared with current assets such as cash or bank accounts, which are described as liquid assets. In most cases, only tangible assets are referred to as fixed.

   a. Bankruptcy prediction
   b. Minority interest
   c. Fixed Asset
   d. Subledger

18. In economic models, the _____ time frame assumes no fixed factors of production. Firms can enter or leave the marketplace, and the cost (and availability) of land, labor, raw materials, and capital goods can be assumed to vary. In contrast, in the short-run time frame, certain factors are assumed to be fixed, because there is not sufficient time for them to change.

   a. BMC Software, Inc.
   b. Short-run
   c. 3M Company
   d. Long-run

19. In finance, a _____ is a debt security, in which the authorized issuer owes the holders a debt and, depending on the terms of the _____, is obliged to pay interest (the coupon) and/or to repay the principal at a later date, termed maturity. It is a formal contract to repay borrowed money with interest at fixed intervals.

   Thus a _____ is like a loan: the issuer is the borrower, the _____ holder is the lender, and the coupon is the interest.

   a. Coupon rate
   b. Bond
   c. Zero-coupon bond
   d. Revenue bonds

20. _____ are financial bonds that mature in installments over a period of time. In effect, a $100,000, 5-year serial bond would mature in a $20,000 annuity over a 5-year interval. Bond issues consisting of a series of blocks of securities maturing in sequence, the coupon rate can be different.

   a. Low Income Housing Tax Credit
   b. Just-in-time
   c. Household and Dependent Care Credit
   d. Serial bonds

21. _____ are sometimes the same as net worth, or shareholders' equity - assets minus liabilities. The term _____ is commonly used with charities or not for profit entities. Although these entities don't make money, it is important to maintain reasonable reserves to help future growth.

   a. Net interest spread
   b. Net assets
   c. Debtor days
   d. Sortino ratio

Chapter 18. Introduction to Accounting for State and Local Governmental Units

22. _____ is the term used in the United States to designate a unique charge government units can assess against real estate parcels for certain public projects. This charge is levied in a specific geographic area known as a _____ District (S.A.D.). A _____ may only be levied against parcels of real estate which have been identified as having received a direct and unique 'benefit' from the public project.Kadzban v City of Grandville, 502 N.W.2d 299, 501; Davies v City of Lawrence, 218 Kan.

    a. Fixed tax
    b. Special assessment
    c. Tax Analysts
    d. Malcolm Baldrige National Quality Award

23. A _____ is a type of debt Like all debt instruments, a _____ entails the redistribution of financial assets over time, between the lender and the borrower.

    a. Loan to value
    b. Lender
    c. Debenture
    d. Loan

Chapter 19. Accounting for Nongovernment Nonbusiness Organizations

1. An _____ is a practitioner of accountancy, which is the measurement, disclosure or provision of assurance about financial information that helps managers, investors, tax authorities and other decision makers make resource allocation decisions.

The word '_____' is derived from the French 'Compter' which took its origin from the Latin 'Computare'. The word was formerly written in English as 'Accomptant', but in process of time the word, which was always pronounced by dropping the 'p', became gradually changed both in pronunciation and in orthography to its present form.

 a. ABC Television Network   b. AIG
 c. Accountant   d. AMEX

2. The _____ is the national, professional association of CPAs in the United States, with more than 330,000 members, including CPAs in business and industry, public practice, government, and education; student affiliates; and international associates. It sets ethical standards for the profession and U.S. auditing standards for audits of private companies; federal, state and local governments; and non-profit organizations.

Approximately 40% of its members are engaged in the practice of public accounting, in areas such as auditing, accounting, taxation, general business consulting, business valuation, personal financial planning and business technology.

 a. American Institute of Certified Public Accountants   b. AIG
 c. ABC Television Network   d. Other postemployment benefits

3. The general definition of an _____ is an evaluation of a person, organization, system, process, project or product. _____s are performed to ascertain the validity and reliability of information; also to provide an assessment of a system's internal control. The goal of an _____ is to express an opinion on the person/organization/system (etc) in question, under evaluation based on work done on a test basis.

 a. Audit   b. Institute of Chartered Accountants of India
 c. Assurance service   d. Audit regime

4. _____ is the statutory title of qualified accountants in the United States who have passed the Uniform _____ Examination and have met additional state education and experience requirements for certification as a _____. Individuals who have passed the Exam but have not either accomplished the required on-the-job experience or have previously met it but in the meantime have lapsed their continuing professional education are, in many states, permitted the designation '_____ Inactive' or an equivalent phrase. In most U.S. states, only _____s who are licensed are able to provide to the public attestation (including auditing) opinions on financial statements.

 a. Certified General Accountant   b. Chartered Certified Accountant
 c. Chartered Accountant   d. Certified Public Accountant

5. _____ is the term used to refer to the standard framework of guidelines for financial accounting used in any given jurisdiction. _____ includes the standards, conventions, and rules accountants follow in recording and summarizing transactions, and in the preparation of financial statements.

Financial accounting information must be assembled and reported objectively.

Chapter 19. Accounting for Nongovernment Nonbusiness Organizations

a. Current asset
b. Generally accepted accounting principles
c. Long-term liabilities
d. General ledger

6. _____ of something is, in finance, the adding together of interest or different investments over a period of time such as atoms (1 - the act or process of accruing; 2 - the amount that accrues.) It holds specific meanings in accounting and payroll.

_____, in accounting, describes the accounting method known as _____ basis, whereby revenues and expenses are recognized when they are accrued, i.e. accumulated (earned or incurred), regardless when the actual cash is received or paid out.

a. Accounts receivable
b. Assets
c. Earnings before interest, taxes, depreciation and amortization
d. Accrual

7. _____ is a method of accounting whereby economic activities (rather than cash flow) of financial events are considered, because of two complementary principles, which (together) determine the point, at which expenses and revenues are recognized. According to revenue recognition principle, revenues are realized when earned, whether or not they are received in cash.

a. Earnings before interest, taxes, depreciation and amortization
b. Accrual
c. Accrued revenue
d. Accrual basis accounting

8. _____ is financial assistance paid to people by governments. Some _____ is general, while specific and can only be invoked under certain circumstances, such as a scholarship. _____ payments can be made to individuals or to companies or entities--these latter payments are often considered corporate _____.

a. Swap
b. Joseph Ronald Banister
c. Price-to-sales ratio
d. Welfare

9. The _____ is a private, not-for-profit organization whose primary purpose is to develop generally accepted accounting principles (GAAP) within the United States in the public's interest. The Securities and Exchange Commission (SEC) designated the _____ as the organization responsible for setting accounting standards for public companies in the U.S. It was created in 1973, replacing the Accounting Principles Board and the Committee on Accounting Procedure of the American Institute of Certified Public Accountants. The _____'s mission is 'to establish and improve standards of financial accounting and reporting for the guidance and education of the public, including issuers, auditors, and users of financial information.'

The _____ is not a governmental body.

a. Fannie Mae
b. Public company
c. Governmental Accounting Standards Board
d. Financial Accounting Standards Board

10. _____ are sometimes the same as net worth, or shareholders' equity - assets minus liabilities. The term _____ is commonly used with charities or not for profit entities. Although these entities don't make money, it is important to maintain reasonable reserves to help future growth.

a. Sortino ratio
b. Net assets
c. Net interest spread
d. Debtor days

11. In business and accounting, _____ are everything of value that is owned by a person or company. It is a claim on the property your income of a borrower. The balance sheet of a firm records the monetary value of the _____ owned by the firm.

a. Accrual basis accounting
b. Accounts receivable
c. Earnings before interest, taxes, depreciation and amortization
d. Assets

12. The _____ is currently the source of generally accepted accounting principles (GAAP) used by State and Local governments in the [[United States of America]]. As with most of the entities involved in creating GAAP in the United States, it is a private, non-governmental organization.

The _____ is subject to oversight by the Financial Accounting Foundation (FAF), which selects the members of the _____ and the Financial Accounting Standards Board, and funds both organizations.

a. Fannie Mae
b. Multinational corporation
c. National Conference of Commissioners on Uniform State Laws
d. Governmental Accounting Standards Board

13. _____ are formal records of a business' financial activities.

In British English, including United Kingdom company law, _____ are often referred to as accounts, although the term _____ is also used, particularly by accountants.

_____ provide an overview of a business' financial condition in both short and long term.

a. Notes to the financial statements
b. 3M Company
c. Statement of retained earnings
d. Financial statements

14. _____ is an accounting system often used by nonprofit organizations and by the public sector. According to StartHereGoPlaces, _____ is a '[m]ethod of accounting and presentation whereby assets and liabilities are grouped according to the purpose for which they are to be used.'

_____ serves any nonprofit organization or the public sector. These organizations have a need for special reporting to financial statements users that show how money is spent, rather than how much profit was earned.

a. Refunding
b. Liquidating dividend
c. Fund accounting
d. Replacement cost

15. A _____ is a type of debt Like all debt instruments, a _____ entails the redistribution of financial assets over time, between the lender and the borrower.

a. Loan
b. Loan to value
c. Debenture
d. Lender

Chapter 19. Accounting for Nongovernment Nonbusiness Organizations

16. The term _____ is used in finance theory to refer to any terminating stream of fixed payments over a specified period of time. This usage is most commonly seen in academic discussions of finance, usually in connection with the valuation of the stream of payments, taking into account time value of money concepts such as interest rate and future value.

Examples of these are regular deposits to a savings account, monthly home mortgage payments and monthly insurance payments.

   a. Annuity
   b. Appropriation
   c. Intangible
   d. Improvement

17. The _____ is the former authoritative body of the American Institute of Certified Public Accountants (AICPA.) It was created by the American Institute of Certified Public Accountants in 1959 and issued pronouncements on accounting principles until 1973, when it was replaced by the Financial Accounting Standards Board (FASB.)

The _____ was disbanded in the hopes that the smaller, fully-independent FASB could more effectively create accounting standards.

   a. International Federation of Accountants
   b. American Payroll Association
   c. Institute of Management Accountants
   d. Accounting Principles Board

18. _____ were published by Accounting Principles Board (APB.) The board was created by American Institute of Certified Public Accountants (AICPA) in 1959 and was replaced by Financial Accounting Standards Board (FASB) in 1973. Its mission was to develop an overall conceptual framework of US generally accepted accounting principles (US GAAP.)

   a. AIG
   b. Accounting Principles Board Opinions
   c. AMEX
   d. ABC Television Network

19. In accounting/accountancy, _____ are journal entries usually made at the end of an accounting period to allocate income and expenditure to the period in which they actually occurred. The revenue recognition principle is the basis of making _____ that pertain to unearned and accrued revenues under accrual-basis accounting. They are sometimes called Balance Day adjustments because they are made on balance day.

   a. Accrual
   b. Accrued expense
   c. Adjusting entries
   d. Earnings before interest, taxes, depreciation and amortization

20. An American Depository Receipt (or _____) represents the ownership in the shares of a foreign company trading on US financial markets. The stock of many non-US companies trades on US exchanges through the use of _____s. American Depository Receiptss enable US investors to buy shares in foreign companies without undertaking cross-border transactions.

   a. American Depository Receipts
   b. AMEX
   c. AIG
   d. ABC Television Network

Chapter 19. Accounting for Nongovernment Nonbusiness Organizations

21. _____ is the act of taking possession of or assigning purpose to properties or ideas and is important in many topics, including:

- _____ in relation to the spread of knowledge
- _____ (art)
   - _____ (music) in reference to the re-use and proliferation of different types of music
- _____ (economics) origination of human ownership of previously unowned natural resources such as land
- _____ (law) as a component of government spending
- Cultural _____ is the borrowing, or theft, of an element of cultural expression of one group by another.
- The tort of _____ is one form of invasion of privacy.

a. Improvement
b. Annuity
c. Intangible
d. Appropriation

22. _____ is a voluntary contract between two or among more than two persons to place their capital, labor, and skills, and corporation in business with the understanding that there will be a sharing of the profits and losses between/among partners. Outside of North America, it is normally referred to simply as a partnership agreement.

There are also multiple sections which are often included as well in _____, based on the circumstance.

a. ABC Television Network
b. AMEX
c. AIG
d. Articles of partnership

23. In accounting, _____ or carrying value is the value of an asset according to its balance sheet account balance. For assets, the value is based on the original cost of the asset less any depreciation, amortization or impairment costs made against the asset. Traditionally, a company's _____ is its total assets minus intangible assets and liabilities.

a. Matching principle
b. Generally accepted accounting principles
c. Depreciation
d. Book value

24. In economics, _____ or _____ goods or real _____ refers to factors of production used to create goods or services that are not themselves significantly consumed (though they may depreciate) in the production process. _____ goods may be acquired with money or financial _____. In finance and accounting, _____ generally refers to financial wealth, especially that used to start or maintain a business.

a. Disclosure
b. Screening
c. Vyborg Appeal
d. Capital

25. A _____ is a type of business entity in which partners (owners) share with each other the profits or losses of the business undertaking in which all have invested. _____s are often favored over corporations for taxation purposes, as the _____ structure does not generally incur a tax on profits before it is distributed to the partners (i.e. there is no dividend tax levied.) However, depending on the _____ structure and the jurisdiction in which it operates, owners of a _____ may be exposed to greater personal liability than they would as shareholders of a corporation.

a. Partnership
b. National Information Infrastructure Protection Act
c. Corporate governance
d. Resource Conservation and Recovery Act

Chapter 19. Accounting for Nongovernment Nonbusiness Organizations

26. An _____ is the buying of one company by another. An _____ may be friendly or hostile. In the former case, the companies cooperate in negotiations; in the latter case, the takeover target is unwilling to be bought or the target's board has no prior knowledge of the offer. _____ usually refers to a purchase of a smaller firm by a larger one. Sometimes, however, a smaller firm will acquire management control of a larger or longer established company and keep its name for the combined entity. This is known as a reverse takeover.

   a. ABC Television Network   b. AIG
   c. Acquisition   d. AMEX

27. _____ is the term used in the United States to designate a unique charge government units can assess against real estate parcels for certain public projects. This charge is levied in a specific geographic area known as a _____ District (S.A.D.). A _____ may only be levied against parcels of real estate which have been identified as having received a direct and unique 'benefit' from the public project.Kadzban v City of Grandville, 502 N.W.2d 299, 501; Davies v City of Lawrence, 218 Kan.

   a. Malcolm Baldrige National Quality Award   b. Fixed tax
   c. Tax Analysts   d. Special assessment

28. In finance, a _____ is a debt security, in which the authorized issuer owes the holders a debt and, depending on the terms of the _____, is obliged to pay interest (the coupon) and/or to repay the principal at a later date, termed maturity. It is a formal contract to repay borrowed money with interest at fixed intervals.

Thus a _____ is like a loan: the issuer is the borrower, the _____ holder is the lender, and the coupon is the interest.

   a. Revenue bonds   b. Coupon rate
   c. Bond   d. Zero-coupon bond

29. _____ is a specific term used in companies' financial reporting from the company-whole point of view. Because that use excludes the effects of changing ownership interest, an economic measure of _____ is necessary for financial analysis from the shareholders' point of view

_____ is defined by the Financial Accounting Standards Board, or FASB, as 'the change in equity [net assets] of a business enterprise during a period from transactions and other events and circumstances from nonowner sources. It includes all changes in equity during a period except those resulting from investments by owners and distributions to owners.'

_____ is the sum of net income and other items that must bypass the income statement because they have not been realized, including items like an unrealized holding gain or loss from available for sale securities and foreign currency translation gains or losses.

   a. BNSF Railway   b. 3M Company
   c. Comprehensive income   d. BMC Software, Inc.

30. _____ are financial statements that factor the holding company's subsidiaries into its aggregated accounting figure. It is a representation of how the holding company is doing as a group. The consolidated accounts should provide a true and fair view of the financial and operating conditions of the group.

Chapter 19. Accounting for Nongovernment Nonbusiness Organizations

a. Committee on Accounting Procedure
b. Consolidated financial statements
c. Redemption value
d. Replacement cost

31. _____ is a common concept in economics, and gives rise to derived concepts such as consumer debt. Generally _____ is defined by opposition to production. But the precise definition can vary because different schools of economists define production quite differently.
   a. Mitigating Control
   b. Consumption
   c. Yield
   d. Starving the beast

32. In economics, business, retail, and accounting, a _____ is the value of money that has been used up to produce something, and hence is not available for use anymore. In economics, a _____ is an alternative that is given up as a result of a decision. In business, the _____ may be one of acquisition, in which case the amount of money expended to acquire it is counted as _____.
   a. Cost allocation
   b. Cost of quality
   c. Cost
   d. Prime cost

33. In finance, the _____ between two currencies specifies how much one currency is worth in terms of the other. It is the value of a foreign nation's currency in terms of the home nation's currency. For example an _____ of 102 Japanese yen to the United States dollar means that JPY 102 is worth the same as USD 1.
   a. ABC Television Network
   b. Exchange rate
   c. AMEX
   d. AIG

34. _____ in accounting is the process of treating equity investments, usually 20-50%, in associate companies. The investor keeps such equities as an asset. Proportional share of associate company's net income increases the investment, and proportional payment of dividends decreases it.
   a. ABC Television Network
   b. AIG
   c. Out-of-pocket
   d. Equity method

35. _____ is a fee paid on borrowed assets. It is the price paid for the use of borrowed money, or, money earned by deposited funds. Assets that are sometimes lent with _____ include money, shares, consumer goods through hire purchase, major assets such as aircraft, and even entire factories in finance lease arrangements. The _____ is calculated upon the value of the assets in the same manner as upon money.
   a. Interest
   b. Insolvency
   c. AIG
   d. ABC Television Network

36. _____ is equal to the income that a firm has after subtracting costs and expenses from the total revenue. _____ can be distributed among holders of common stock as a dividend or held by the firm as retained earnings.

The items deducted will typically include tax expense, financing expense (interest expense), and minority interest. Likewise, preferred stock dividends will be subtracted too, though they are not an expense.

   a. Matching principle
   b. Generally accepted accounting principles
   c. Long-term liabilities
   d. Net income

Chapter 19. Accounting for Nongovernment Nonbusiness Organizations

37. _____ is that which is owed; usually referencing assets owed, but the term can also cover moral obligations and other interactions not requiring money. In the case of assets, _____ is a means of using future purchasing power in the present before a summation has been earned. Some companies and corporations use _____ as a part of their overall corporate finance strategy.
   a. Lender
   b. Loan
   c. Debt
   d. Debenture

38. _____, in accrual accounting, is any account where the asset or liability is not realized until a future date (accounting period), e.g. annuities, charges, taxes, income, etc. The _____ item may be carried, dependent on type of deferral, as either an asset or liability.
   a. Payroll
   b. Cash basis accounting
   c. Pro forma
   d. Deferred

39. _____ is an accounting concept, meaning a future tax liability or asset, resulting from temporary differences between book (accounting) value of assets and liabilities and their tax value, or timing differences between the recognition of gains and losses in financial statements and their recognition in a tax computation.

Temporary differences are differences between the carrying amount of an asset or liability recognised in the balance sheet and the amount attributed to that asset or liability for tax purposes (the tax base.)

   a. Federal tax revenue by state
   b. Deferred tax
   c. Tax refund
   d. Deficit

40. In an economy, production, consumption and exchange are carried out by two basic _____: the firm and the household.
   a. AIG
   b. Economic units
   c. ABC Television Network
   d. AMEX

41. _____ is a legal term of art for anything that affects or limits the title of a property, such as mortgages, leases, easements, liens, or restrictions. Also, those considered as potentially making the title defeasible are also _____s. For example, charging orders, building orders and structure alteration.
   a. Ownership
   b. ABC Television Network
   c. Administrative proceeding
   d. Encumbrance

42. In accounting, _____ has a very specific meaning. It is an outflow of cash or other valuable assets from a person or company to another person or company. This outflow of cash is generally one side of a trade for products or services that have equal or better current or future value to the buyer than to the seller.
   a. AIG
   b. ABC Television Network
   c. AMEX
   d. Expense

43. The _____ duty is a legal relationship of confidence or trust between two or more parties, most commonly a _____ or trustee and a principal or beneficiary. One party, for example a corporate trust company or the trust department of a bank, holds a _____ relation or acts in a _____ capacity to another, such as one whose funds are entrusted to it for investment. In a _____ relation one person justifiably reposes confidence, good faith, reliance and trust in another whose aid, advice or protection is sought in some matter.

94 *Chapter 19. Accounting for Nongovernment Nonbusiness Organizations*

a. Staple right
b. Fiduciary
c. FCPA
d. Robinson-Patman Act

44. _____ is any physical or virtual entity that is owned by an individual or jointly by a group of individuals. An owner of _____ has the right to consume, sell, rent, mortgage, transfer and exchange his or her _____. Important widely-recognized types of _____ include real _____, personal _____ (other physical possessions), and intellectual _____ (rights over artistic creations, inventions, etc.), although the latter is not always as widely recognized or enforced.

a. Property
b. Fiduciary
c. Disclosure requirement
d. Primary authority

45. A _____ is the pinnacle activity involved in selling products or services in return for money or other compensation. It is an act of completion of a commercial activity.

A _____ is completed by the seller, the owner of the goods.

a. Sale
b. Maturity
c. High yield stock
d. Tertiary sector of economy

46. In monetary economics _____ can refer either to a particular _____, for example British Pounds or United States Dollars, or, to the coins and banknotes of a particular _____, which actually form only a small part of the monetary base of a nation's money supply. The other part of a nation's money supply consists of money deposited in banks (sometimes called deposit money), ownership of which can be transferred by means of checks (cheques in the United Kingdom and Australia) or other forms of money transfer such as credit and debit cards. Deposit money and _____ are 'money' in the sense that both are acceptable as a means of exchange, but money need not necessarily be '_____'.

a. BMC Software, Inc.
b. Currency
c. 3M Company
d. BNSF Railway

47. _____, also known as property, plant, and equipment (PP&E), is a term used in accountancy for assets and property which cannot easily be converted into cash. This can be compared with current assets such as cash or bank accounts, which are described as liquid assets. In most cases, only tangible assets are referred to as fixed.

a. Bankruptcy prediction
b. Minority interest
c. Subledger
d. Fixed Asset

48. _____ is the monetary unit of account of the principal economic environment in which an economic entity operates.

Statement of Financial Standards No. 52 (SFAS 52) is the primary source of GAAP for translation of foreign currency financial statements.

a. BMC Software, Inc.
b. 3M Company
c. BNSF Railway
d. Functional currency

Chapter 19. Accounting for Nongovernment Nonbusiness Organizations

49. In the commercial and legal parlance of most countries, a _____ or simply a partnership, refers to an association of persons or an unincorporated company with the following major features:

- Created by agreement, proof of existence and estoppel.
- Formed by two or more persons
- The owners are all personally liable for any legal actions and debts the company may face

It is a partnership in which partners share equally in both responsibility and liability.

Partnerships have certain default characteristics relating to both the relationship between the individual partners and (b) the relationship between the partnership and the outside world. The former can generally be overridden by agreement between the partners, whereas the latter generally cannot be.

The assets of the business are owned on behalf of the other partners, and they are each personally liable, jointly and severally, for business debts, taxes or tortious liability.

a. Dow Jones ' Company
b. General partnership
c. Multinational corporation
d. Governmental Accounting Standards Board

50. _____ is an umbrella term which refers to the various accounting systems used by various public sector entities. In the United States, for instance, there are two levels of government which follow different accounting standards set forth by independent, private sector boards. At the federal level, the Federal Accounting Standards Advisory Board (FASAB) sets forth the accounting standards to follow.

a. Management accounting
b. Nonassurance services
c. Product control
d. Governmental accounting

51. In economic models, the _____ time frame assumes no fixed factors of production. Firms can enter or leave the marketplace, and the cost (and availability) of land, labor, raw materials, and capital goods can be assumed to vary. In contrast, in the short-run time frame, certain factors are assumed to be fixed, because there is not sufficient time for them to change.

a. BMC Software, Inc.
b. Short-run
c. Long-run
d. 3M Company

52. _____, also called fair price (in a commonplace conflation of the two distinct concepts), is a concept used in finance and economics, defined as a rational and unbiased estimate of the potential market price of a good, service, or asset, taking into account such objective factors as:

- acquisition/production/distribution costs, replacement costs, or costs of close substitutes
- actual utility at a given level of development of social productive capability
- supply vs. demand

and subjective factors such as

- risk characteristics
- cost of capital
- individually perceived utility

In accounting, _____ is used as an estimate of the market value of an asset (or liability) for which a market price cannot be determined (usually because there is no established market for the asset.) Under GAAP (FAS 157), _____ is the amount at which the asset could be bought or sold in a current transaction between willing parties, or transferred to an equivalent party, other than in a liquidation sale. This is used for assets whose carrying value is based on mark-to-market valuations; for assets carried at historical cost, the _____ of the asset is not used. One example of where _____ is an issue is a College kitchen with a cost of $2 million which was built 5 years ago.

    a. BNSF Railway
    b. Fair value
    c. 3M Company
    d. BMC Software, Inc.

53. An _____ is a term used in behavioral economics to describe those types of behaviors that impose costs on a person in the long-run that are not taken into account when making decisions in the present. Classical Economics discourages government from creating legislation that targets internalities, because it is assumed that the consumer takes these personal costs into account when paying for the good that causes the _____. For example, cigarettes should be taxed because of the negative consumption externalities that they impose, such as second-hand smoke, not because the smoker harms him or herself by smoking.

    a. Inventory turnover ratio
    b. Authorised capital
    c. Operating budget
    d. Internality

54. _____ was founded in June 1973 in London and replaced by the International Accounting Standards Board on April 1, 2001. It was responsible for developing the International Accounting Standards and promoting the use and application of these standards.

Chapter 19. Accounting for Nongovernment Nonbusiness Organizations

The _____ was founded as a result of an agreement between accountancy bodies in the following countries:

- Australia (Institute of Chartered Accountants in Australia (ICAA) and the CPA Australia (formerly known as Australian Society of Certified Practising Accountants (ASCPA))

- Canada (Canadian Institute of Chartered Accountants (CICA))

- France (Ordre des Experts Comptable et des Comptables Agrees (Order of Accounting Experts and Qualified Accountants))

- Germany and the Wirtschaftsprüferkammer (WPK) (Chamber of Auditors))

- Japan Nihon Kouninkaikeishi Kyoukai)

- Mexico (Instituto Mexicano de Contadores Publicos (IMCP) (Mexican Institute of Public Accountants)) (removed from the board in 1987 due to non-payment of dues; resumed in 1995.)

- the Netherlands (Nederlands Instituut van Registeraccountants (NIVRA)

(Netherlands Institute of Registered Auditors))

- the United Kingdom and Ireland (counted as one) (Institute of Chartered Accountants in England and Wales (ICAEW), Institute of Chartered Accountants of Scotland (ICAS), Institute of Chartered Accountants in Ireland (ICAI), Association of Certified Accountants, Institute of Cost and Management Accountants, and the Institute of Municipal Treasurers and Accountants)

- the United States of America (American Institute of Certified Public Accountants (AICPA))

The Institute of Chartered Accountants of Nigeria became an associate member in 1976 and a member of the board from 1978 to 1987.

The National Council of Chartered Accountants (South Africa) became an associate member in 1974 and joined the board in 1978.

a. International Accounting Standards Committee
b. American Accounting Association
c. American Payroll Association
d. International Accounting Standards Board

55. The _____ is the global organization for the accountancy profession. IFAC has 157 member bodies and associates in 123 countries and jurisdictions, representing more than 2.5 million accountants employed in public practice, industry and commerce, government, and academe. The organization, through its independent standard-setting boards, establishes international standards on ethics, auditing and assurance, education, and public sector accounting.

a. American Payroll Association
b. International Federation of Accountants
c. Emerging technologies
d. International Accounting Standards Committee

Chapter 19. Accounting for Nongovernment Nonbusiness Organizations

56. A _____ is an entity formed between two or more parties to undertake economic activity together. The parties agree to create a new entity by both contributing equity, and they then share in the revenues, expenses, and control of the enterprise. The venture can be for one specific project only, or a continuing business relationship such as the Fuji Xerox _____.
   a. Joint venture
   b. Pre-emption right
   c. Fraud Enforcement and Recovery Act
   d. Chief Financial Officers Act of 1990

57. A _____ occurs when a financial sponsor acquires a controlling interest in a company's equity and where a significant percentage of the purchase price is financed through leverage (borrowing.) The assets of the acquired company are used as collateral for the borrowed capital, sometimes with assets of the acquiring company. The bonds or other paper issued for a _____ is commonly considered not to be investment grade because of the significant risks involved.
   a. BNSF Railway
   b. 3M Company
   c. BMC Software, Inc.
   d. Leveraged buyout

58. A _____ is a form of partnership similar to a general partnership, except that in addition to one or more general partners (GPs), there are one or more limited partners (_____s.) It is a partnership in which only one partner is required to be a general partner.

The GPs are, in all major respects, in the same legal position as partners in a conventional firm, i.e. they have management control, share the right to use partnership property, share the profits of the firm in predefined proportions, and have joint and several liability for the debts of the partnership.

   a. Dow Jones ' Company
   b. Debenture
   c. Limited partnership
   d. Minority interest

59. _____ is a payment of a dividend to stockholders that exceeds the company's retained earnings. Once retained earnings is depleted, capital accounts such as additional paid-in capital are decreased to make up for the remaining dividend to be paid to stockholders. When a _____ occurs, it is considered to be a return of investment instead of profits.
   a. Fund accounting
   b. Trade name
   c. Redemption value
   d. Liquidating dividend

60. In law, _____ refers to the process by which a company (or part of a company) is brought to an end, and the assets and property of the company redistributed. _____ can also be referred to as winding-up or dissolution, although dissolution technically refers to the last stage of _____. The process of _____ also arises when customs, an authority or agency in a country responsible for collecting and safeguarding customs duties, determines the final computation or ascertainment of the duties or drawback accruing on an entry.
   a. BMC Software, Inc.
   b. Bankruptcy protection
   c. Liquidation
   d. 3M Company

61. In economics, a _____, in its common usage, is a currency not backed by a national government (and not necessarily legal tender), and intended to trade only in a small area. These currencies are also referred to as community currency, or complementary currency. They encompass a wide range of forms, both physically and financially, and often are associated with a particular economic discourse.

Chapter 19. Accounting for Nongovernment Nonbusiness Organizations

a. Local currency
c. BNSF Railway
b. 3M Company
d. BMC Software, Inc.

62. _____ is the state or fact of exclusive rights and control over property, which may be an object, land/real estate or intellectual property. An _____ right is also referred to as title.

_____ is the key building block in the development of the capitalist socio-economic system.

a. Administrative proceeding
c. Ownership
b. ABC Television Network
d. Encumbrance

63. A _____, in business matters, is an entity that is controlled by a bigger and more powerful entity. The controlled entity is called a company, corporation, or limited liability company, and the controlling entity is called its parent (or the parent company.) The reason for this distinction is that a lone company cannot be a _____ of any organization; only an entity representing a legal fiction as a separate entity can be a _____.

a. 3M Company
c. Parent company
b. BMC Software, Inc.
d. Subsidiary

64. _____ are payments made by a corporation to its shareholder members. It is the portion of corporate profits paid out to stockholders. When a corporation earns a profit or surplus, that money can be put to two uses: it can either be re-invested in the business (called retained earnings), or it can be paid to the shareholders as a dividend.

a. Dividend stripping
c. Dividend payout ratio
b. Dividend yield
d. Dividends

65. Employment is a contract between two parties, one being the employer and the other being the _____. An _____ may be defined as: 'A person in the service of another under any contract of hire, express or implied, oral or written, where the employer has the power or right to control and direct the _____ in the material details of how the work is to be performed.' Black's Law Dictionary page 471 (5th ed. 1979.)

a. AMEX
c. AIG
b. ABC Television Network
d. Employee

66. _____ in business is an accounting concept that refers to ownership of a company (subsidiary) that is less than 50% of outstanding shares. _____ belongs to other investors and is reported on the consolidated balance sheet of the owning company to reflect the claim on assets belonging to other, non-controlling shareholders. Also, _____ is reported on the consolidated income statement as a share of profit belonging to minority shareholders.

a. Subledger
c. Credit memo
b. Bankruptcy prediction
d. Minority interest

67. In finance, an _____ is a contract between a buyer and a seller that gives the buyer the right--but not the obligation-- to buy or to sell a particular asset (the underlying asset) at a later time at an agreed price. In return for granting the _____, the seller collects a payment (the premium) from the buyer. A call _____ gives the buyer the right to buy the underlying asset; a put _____ gives the buyer of the _____ the right to sell the underlying asset.

a. AIG
c. ABC Television Network
b. AMEX
d. Option

Chapter 19. Accounting for Nongovernment Nonbusiness Organizations

68. A _____ is a company that owns enough voting stock in another firm to control management and operations by influencing or electing its board of directors; the second company being deemed as a subsidiary of the _____. The definition of a _____ differs from jurisdiction to jurisdiction, with the definition normally being defined by way of laws dealing with companies in that jurisdiction.

The _____-subsidiary company relationship is defined by Part 1.2, Division 6, Section 46 of the Corporations Act 2001 (Cth), which states:

A body corporate (in this section called the first body) is a subsidiary of another body corporate if, and only if:

(a) the other body:

(i) controls the composition of the first body's board; or

(ii) is in a position to cast, or control the casting of, more than one-half of the maximum number of votes that might be cast at a general meeting of the first body; or

(iii) holds more than one-half of the issued share capital of the first body (excluding any part of that issued share capital that carries no right to participate beyond a specified amount in a distribution of either profits or capital); or

(b) the first body is a subsidiary of a subsidiary of the other body.

a. Subsidiary
b. BMC Software, Inc.
c. 3M Company
d. Parent company

69. The term _____ is a term applied to practices that are perfunctory, or seek to satisfy the minimum requirements or to conform to a convention or doctrine. It has different meanings in different fields.

In accounting, _____ earnings are those earnings of companies in addition to actual earnings calculated under the Generally Accepted Accounting Principles (GAAP) in their quarterly and yearly financial reports.

a. Treasury stock
b. Pro forma
c. Payroll
d. Bottom line

70. The word _____ indicates that a party, or proprietor, exercises private ownership, control or use over an item of property
a. 3M Company
b. BNSF Railway
c. BMC Software, Inc.
d. Proprietary

71. The spot price or _____ of a commodity, a security or a currency is the price that is quoted for immediate (spot) settlement (payment and delivery.) Spot settlement is normally one or two business days from trade date. This is in contrast with the forward price established in a forward contract or futures contract, where contract terms (price) are set now, but delivery and payment will occur at a future date.

Chapter 19. Accounting for Nongovernment Nonbusiness Organizations 101

   a. Market price
   c. Financial instruments
   b. Market liquidity
   d. Spot rate

72. _____ is a measure of a company's earning power from ongoing operations, equal to earnings before the deduction of interest payments and income taxes.

To accountants, economic profit, or EP, is a single-period metric to determine the value created by a company in one period - usually a year. It is the net profit after tax less the equity charge, a risk-weighted cost of capital.

   a. ABC Television Network
   c. AMEX
   b. AIG
   d. Operating profit

73. A _____ is the transfer of wealth from one party (such as a person or company) to another. A _____ is usually made in exchange for the provision of goods, services or both, or to fulfill a legal obligation.

The simplest and oldest form of _____ is barter, the exchange of one good or service for another.

   a. BMC Software, Inc.
   c. Payee
   b. 3M Company
   d. Payment

74. _____ refers to a business or organization attempting to acquire goods or services to accomplish the goals of the enterprise. Though there are several organizations that attempt to set standards in the _____ process, processes can vary greatly between organizations. Typically the word e;_____e; is not used interchangeably with the word e;procuremente;, since procurement typically includes Expediting, Supplier Quality, and Traffic and Logistics (T'L) in addition to _____.

   a. Supply chain
   c. Consignor
   b. Purchasing
   d. Free port

75. _____ is an SEC filing submitted to the US Securities and Exchange Commission used by certain foreign private issuers to provide information.

20-F, 20-F/A Annual and transition report of foreign private issuers pursuant to sections 13 or 15(d)

20FR12B, 20FR12B/A Form for initial registration of a class of securities of foreign private issuers pursuant to section 12(b)

20FR12G, 20FR12G/A Form for initial registration of a class of securities of foreign private issuers pursuant to section 12(g)

The postfix /A stands for 'Amendment'

The report must be filed within six months after the end of the fiscal year.

Chapter 19. Accounting for Nongovernment Nonbusiness Organizations

a. Form 10-Q
b. 3M Company
c. Form 8-K
d. Form 20-F

76. In financial accounting, a _____ is defined as an obligation of an entity arising from past transactions or events, the settlement of which may result in the transfer or use of assets, provision of services or other yielding of economic benefits in the future.
   a. Liability
   b. False Claims Act
   c. Vested
   d. Corporate governance

77. In business or economics a _____ is a combination of two companies into one larger company. Such actions are commonly voluntary and involve stock swap or cash payment to the target. Stock swap is often used as it allows the shareholders of the two companies to share the risk involved in the deal. A _____ can resemble a takeover but result in a new company name (often combining the names of the original companies) and in new branding; in some cases, terming the combination a '_____' rather than an acquisition is done purely for political or marketing reasons.
   a. BNSF Railway
   b. Merger
   c. 3M Company
   d. BMC Software, Inc.

78. _____ is one of the four Ps of the marketing mix. The other three aspects are product, promotion, and place. It is also a key variable in microeconomic price allocation theory.
   a. Target costing
   b. Pricing
   c. Cost-plus pricing
   d. Price

79. A _____, (formerly a securities exchange) is a corporation or mutual organization which provides 'trading' facilities for stock brokers and traders, to trade stocks and other securities. _____s also provide facilities for the issue and redemption of securities as well as other financial instruments and capital events including the payment of income and dividends. The securities traded on a _____ include: shares issued by companies, unit trusts, derivatives, pooled investment products and bonds.
   a. BMC Software, Inc.
   b. BNSF Railway
   c. 3M Company
   d. Stock exchange

80. _____ refers to the pricing of contributions (assets, tangible and intangible, services, and funds) transferred within an organization. For example, goods from the production division may be sold to the marketing division, or goods from a parent company may be sold to a foreign subsidiary. Since the prices are set within an organization (i.e. controlled), the typical market mechanisms that establish prices for such transactions between third parties may not apply.
   a. Price
   b. Pricing
   c. Transfer pricing
   d. Transactional Net Margin Method

81. A _____ or reacquired stock is stock which is bought back by the issuing company, reducing the amount of outstanding stock on the open market ('open market' including insiders' holdings).

Stock repurchases are often used as a tax-efficient method to put cash into shareholders' hands, rather than pay dividends. Sometimes, companies do this when they feel that their stock is undervalued on the open market.

   a. Matching principle
   b. Cost of goods sold
   c. Net profit
   d. Treasury stock

Chapter 19. Accounting for Nongovernment Nonbusiness Organizations

82. The _____ , which includes revisions that are sometimes called the Revised _____ , is a uniform act (similar to a model statute), proposed by the National Conference of Commissioners on Uniform State Laws ('NCCUSL') for the governance of business partnerships by U.S. States. Several versions of _____ have been promulgated by the NCCUSL, the earliest having been put forth in 1914, and the most recent in 1997.

The NCCUSL's first revision of _____ was promulgated in 1992 and amended in 1993 and 1994.

a. AMEX
c. ABC Television Network
b. Uniform Partnership Act
d. AIG

83. _____ is generally understood in financial circles as the point at which revenue is recognized, typically through a transaction which involves the exchange of an asset, product, or service for cash or its equivalents.

This approach gives the accounting division a strictly objective basis for changing the books. For example, a homeowner may believe that his house has grown in value during a strong market, or fallen in value during a weak market, but until the house is actually sold for a specific price to a specific buyer, the change in value can only be estimated and is considered unrealized.

a. Merck ' Co., Inc.
c. Valuation
b. Total-factor productivity
d. Realization

84. In microeconomics and management, the term _____ describes a style of management control. Vertically integrated companies are united through a hierarchy with a common owner. Usually each member of the hierarchy produces a different product or (market-specific) service, and the products combine to satisfy a common need.

a. BMC Software, Inc.
c. BNSF Railway
b. 3M Company
d. Vertical integration

Chapter 1
1. d 2. c 3. d 4. d 5. c 6. d 7. d 8. d 9. a 10. d
11. a 12. d 13. d 14. d 15. d 16. d 17. a 18. a 19. c 20. c
21. a 22. d 23. c 24. c 25. d 26. c 27. c 28. d 29. b 30. b
31. d 32. a 33. a 34. d 35. b

Chapter 2
1. d 2. a 3. c 4. c 5. c 6. d 7. a 8. b 9. c 10. c
11. b 12. d 13. a 14. d 15. a 16. d 17. d 18. d 19. a 20. d
21. d 22. a 23. c 24. a 25. c

Chapter 3
1. d 2. a 3. d 4. d 5. d 6. d 7. b 8. d 9. d 10. d
11. d 12. b 13. d 14. b 15. d 16. d 17. c 18. d 19. c 20. d
21. a 22. d 23. d 24. d 25. a

Chapter 4
1. c 2. d 3. a 4. c 5. b 6. d 7. d 8. d 9. b 10. c
11. d 12. c 13. d 14. c 15. d 16. b 17. c 18. d 19. d 20. d
21. d

Chapter 5
1. c 2. d 3. d 4. d 5. d 6. d 7. d 8. a 9. d 10. d
11. d 12. c 13. d 14. d 15. d 16. d 17. d 18. a 19. c 20. b
21. b 22. a 23. b 24. c 25. d 26. c 27. c 28. a

Chapter 6
1. a 2. b 3. b 4. c 5. d 6. a 7. d 8. d 9. c 10. d
11. d 12. b 13. d 14. d

Chapter 7
1. b 2. d 3. a 4. a 5. d 6. d 7. a 8. d 9. c 10. a
11. d

Chapter 8
1. b 2. d 3. d 4. d 5. d 6. d 7. d 8. d 9. d

Chapter 9
1. d 2. d 3. a 4. b 5. d 6. c 7. c 8. d 9. b 10. c
11. c 12. d 13. d 14. b

Chapter 10
1. a 2. b 3. d 4. c 5. d 6. d 7. a 8. a 9. d 10. a
11. d 12. d 13. c 14. c 15. b 16. b 17. d 18. b 19. d 20. d
21. c

ANSWER KEY

Chapter 11
1. d	2. d	3. d	4. d	5. d	6. a	7. a	8. c	9. d	10. b
11. b	12. d	13. a	14. d	15. d	16. b	17. c	18. b	19. a	20. d
21. a	22. d	23. a	24. b	25. d	26. d	27. d	28. a	29. d	30. b
31. d	32. d	33. d	34. c						

Chapter 12
1. a	2. a	3. a	4. d	5. d	6. d	7. d	8. d	9. c	10. d
11. d	12. d	13. c	14. d	15. d	16. b	17. b	18. b	19. d	20. d
21. a	22. a	23. d	24. d	25. b	26. d	27. a	28. a		

Chapter 13
1. d	2. b	3. c	4. d	5. a	6. d	7. c	8. d	9. d	10. c
11. c	12. c	13. d	14. b	15. c					

Chapter 14
1. d	2. d	3. b	4. a	5. a	6. d	7. c	8. d	9. b	10. b
11. a	12. d	13. d	14. a	15. d	16. d	17. c	18. d	19. d	20. d
21. a	22. d	23. d							

Chapter 15
1. d	2. c	3. c	4. d	5. c	6. d	7. d	8. b	9. d	10. d
11. d	12. d	13. d	14. a	15. d	16. d	17. d			

Chapter 16
1. d	2. d	3. d	4. a	5. b	6. b

Chapter 17
1. d	2. d	3. d	4. a	5. c	6. a	7. d	8. d	9. b	10. a
11. a	12. c	13. a	14. d	15. a	16. a	17. d	18. c	19. d	20. d
21. b	22. d	23. b							

Chapter 18
1. d	2. a	3. d	4. a	5. d	6. b	7. d	8. d	9. d	10. d
11. d	12. b	13. d	14. c	15. c	16. d	17. c	18. d	19. b	20. d
21. b	22. b	23. d							

Chapter 19

1. c	2. a	3. a	4. d	5. b	6. d	7. d	8. d	9. d	10. b
11. d	12. d	13. d	14. c	15. a	16. a	17. d	18. b	19. c	20. a
21. d	22. d	23. d	24. d	25. a	26. c	27. d	28. c	29. c	30. b
31. b	32. c	33. b	34. d	35. a	36. d	37. c	38. d	39. b	40. b
41. d	42. d	43. b	44. a	45. a	46. b	47. d	48. d	49. b	50. d
51. c	52. b	53. d	54. a	55. b	56. a	57. d	58. c	59. d	60. c
61. a	62. c	63. d	64. d	65. d	66. d	67. d	68. d	69. b	70. d
71. d	72. d	73. d	74. b	75. d	76. a	77. b	78. b	79. d	80. c
81. d	82. b	83. d	84. d						

www.ingramcontent.com/pod-product-compliance
Lightning Source LLC
Chambersburg PA
CBHW081844230426
43669CB00018B/2814